Peer Supervision
Beyond the Basics

Handbook For
Spiritual Directors

BY ELLEN TOMASZEWSKI

Peer Supervision – Beyond the Basics
Handbook for Spiritual Directors
Of Ignatian Spirituality

Published by Etcetera Press LLC
Richland, WA

© 2024 E. Tomaszewski

For additional handbooks contact:
Etcetera Press LLC

http://spiritual-exercises.com
Or purchase a copy on Amazon.com

All rights reserved. No part of this book can be copied or reproduced in any way, including digitally.
Please do not make copies of this document for distribution without express written consent from the publisher or author.

Contents

Introduction 5

Section I - Personal Tools for Peers and Presenter

What is Supervision 9
1. Confidentiality 18
2. Two Standards for Supervision 30
3. Worldly Model Expanded 42
4. Christ-Centered Model Expanded 50
5. Affectivity 59
6. Discernment Guidelines 75

Section II - Tools for the Presenter

7. Christ-Centered Model as Presenter 86
8. Transcribing the Direction Session 98
9. Choosing a Session for Supervision 107
10. Writing the Supervision Paper 111
11. The Supervision Session for the Presenter 127

Section III - Tools for Peer Supervisors

12. Christ-Centered Values for Group Members 138
13. Creating the Supervision Environment 145

14 Communication in Christ 154
15 Listening with Heart 160
16 Issues You Might Discover 171
17 Supervision Techniques 181
18 Dealing with Stress 187
19 Consultation 196
20 Conclusion 207

Appendix

Ethical Conduct Guidelines 209
Spiritual Director's Personal Growth 209
Spiritual Director and Directee 210
Spiritual Director and Community 211
Negative Feeling List 212
Positive Feelings List 213
Spiritual Direction Log Form 214
Identifying Your Statement of Intent Form 215
Sample Verbatim Paragraph Style 216
Sample Verbatim Conversation Chart Style 218
Supervision Presentation Form (for presenter) .. 220
Supervision Meeting Agenda 222
About the Author 223
21 Endnotes 227

Introduction

During my first session of my supervision training, I felt so nervous I could barely speak. I prayed that the pounding of my heart wasn't visible. I came to the training with an idea that supervision was important. But after a few sessions, I began to see why supervision makes a difference in my ability to direct a person to God. I learned how important it is to keep my issues from mixing with, influencing, or even blocking a directee's ability to hear God, and how to address them so they won't.

Feeling threatened or nervous about self-revelation is a learned response; we have been taught to protect the ego, sometimes at all costs. But sometimes, those instinctive responses interfere with hearing God speak. As a result, they can disrupt a spiritual director's ability to provide effective spiritual direction and even possibly prevent a person from answering God's invitation to depth.

The spiritual direction supervision process was adapted from supervision in the psychological community. It helps a spiritual director uncover personal agendas, self-protective motives, or psychological and spiritual impediments to freedom in the spiritual director.

Supervision is vital for every spiritual director, new or experienced. It provides an opportunity for a spiritual director (some say companion) to perform a personal inventory, to prayerfully explore personality traits or issues that might interfere with direction, as well as moments of grace, and then use that information to grow and develop into a better person and in the process, become a better spiritual director.

It is important to note that supervision deals with the inner movements of the **_director_**, not the directed. During the process, the director and supervisor(s) contemplatively listen together to God and what has been going on inside the director (his or her **_affect_**) while he/she is listening to another. Both the supervised spiritual director and supervisors explore together where they noticed God in the direction session.

Effective supervision opens the director to self and his or her feelings, responses, or reactions, which might include almost any emotion including boredom, anger, fear, anxiety, distraction, as well as enthusiasm, joy, peace, and hope.

Supervision provides many benefits including:
- Opens the heart and soul more fully to God.
- Increases inner freedom, transparency and humility.
- Aligns human hearts with the work of the Holy Spirit.
- Helps a person hone the ability to be a spiritual director.
- Develops close relationships, trust, and respect among supervision group members.

Here's what supervision is not:
- NOT Spiritual Direction.
- NOT finger-pointing or accusing self or others.
- NOT focused on the directee.
- NOT solving directee or director problems.
- NOT discussable beyond the supervision process.
- NOT a power play or confrontation.
- NOT easy.
- NOT advice-giving.
- NOT a request for, or instructions about the best way to handle a situation, (which is consultation), although it can

include consultation.

Every member of your group must understand and promise to uphold values under which you'll conduct meetings. This means each person will promote Christ-centered, creative openness. And each person will mention to and remind the group whenever the group or individuals in it stray from this Christ-centered openness.

This book will help you begin or improve your spiritual direction through group supervision. It provides formats for recording direction sessions, supervision presentations, verbatim, and a supervision meeting agenda. And hopefully, it will help you grow toward Christ and deepen your prayer.

Section I

Personal Tools for Peers and Presenters

What is Supervision

According to St. John of the Cross, the person wishing to advance toward perfection should "take care into whose hands he entrusts himself, for as the master is, so will the disciple be, and as the father is so will be the son." And further: "In addition to being learned and discreet a director should be experienced in the spiritual life.... If the spiritual director has no experience of the spiritual life, he will be incapable of leading into it the souls whom God is calling to it, and he will not even understand them."[1]

You, as spiritual director, then, will deepen your skills in spiritual direction through practice, education, and especially supervision, where others can assist you in your advance toward perfection. Supervision is not always appreciated by spiritual directors who might see it as invasive or humiliating. But it is an important aspect of spiritual direction that must not be ignored or avoided. Supervision makes the spiritual director humbler, more open, and more able to understand what happens in the spiritual direction session.

Supervision is a method of prayer and evaluation used to help the spiritual director learn how to set him- or herself aside so that, as St. Ignatius puts it, "the Creator can deal directly with the creature" (in this case, the directee.) [See Annotation 15, Spiritual Exercises of St. Ignatius][2]. It is a process that helps us learn to love like God by noticing what's happening in *US* while we direct. This process uses the spiritual direction session as a focus. It is designed to help spiritual directors as well as supervisor(s) notice the subtilties within self. These in turn assist both director and supervisor in personal as well as spiritual growth.

The goal for supervision is to promote and develop self-awareness which in turn fosters inner freedom in the spiritual director. You probably know that you cannot help any directee foster self-awareness if you don't develop the skills to increase your own self-awareness. This is the main point of both spiritual direction and supervision for spiritual directors.

As Maureen Conroy mentions, inner freedom is important also. This freedom allows you as spiritual director to be open, honest, relational, and observant. Sin does not tie down the spiritual director who has the freedom to be open about attachments and other issues that might cause trouble in the direction session. As St. Paul explains in Romans 6:17-18: "***Once you were slaves of sin but thank God you have given whole-hearted obedience to the pattern of teaching to which you were introduced; and so, being freed from serving sin, you took uprightness as your master.***" [3]

I'm sure you know that this doesn't mean we are given license to do what we want or follow our own will. Instead, we are given the freedom to allow God complete control over our lives, especially during spiritual direction and supervision sessions.

Supervision helps us gain freedom by giving the spiritual director a method to evaluate any spiritual direction conversation, looking for places that the spiritual director veered from the focus of God or drew closer. Supervision can reveal where a spiritual director usurped God's role and tried to "fix" things for the directee, or where the spiritual director let God lead.

During a supervision session, the presenter focuses on what's inside his or her own heart, the affectivity that was triggered and why. Supervision is always focused on you, the spiritual director, not the directee.

You as spiritual director need to know what you want in relation to any supervision session. Think about your deepest desires. Do you want to be transparent so God can work better? Perhaps you want to help your directees deepen their prayer life. Maybe you want to get out of God's way so God can work in the heart of your directee easier. Supervision can help you explore those desires and uncover ways to realize them.

Defining Spiritual Direction

As you most likely know, by definition, a spiritual director does not direct people's lives or actions in a worldly way. A spiritual director does not advise on how to keep a house clean, how to be better at the job, how to calm someone's anger, or how to live with dysfunctional family members, for instance. Even if a spiritual director is a therapist with much knowledge of human interaction, giving solutions is not spiritual direction. Spiritual direction is not life coaching, therapy, or leading the directee to certain outcomes. Rather, a spiritual director humbly accompanies a directee into spiritual considerations and prayer. During this process, both directee and director journey toward God together. When a directee forgets to pray, or loses sight of God in the journey, the spiritual director reminds and gently redirects the directee toward God. That's the kind of "direction" we are talking about.

Giving God control over a direction session means the spiritual director releases control over the outcome, increasing trust that God will direct the spiritual director and the directee. This is not always easy to do, nor is it intuitive. To do so, most spiritual directors must first unlearn habitual ways of acting that have been instilled in them by culture, family, school, or life experience. These might include problem-solving, thinking about what you'll say next, or solution-based listening. Supervision helps you, the spiritual director, understand where you've been too self-centered and where you've put God first. Supervision helps every spiritual director unlearn solution-giving (being the guru) and then deepen skills that help direct others toward God.

To say that "refraining from giving solutions or advice" is 'direction' might seem counter intuitive. Life experience teaches us how to overcome various problems and circumstances and direct others in the same process. We develop methods for problem solving and want to share those methods with others who struggle, and often out of kindness or care, direct people to solutions throughout our lives. For instance, parents give advice and life skills instruction to children. Those in the workforce or government are paid to provide solutions for various technical, political or personnel problems. Our culture in general expects solutions for almost any issue.

People who become spiritual directors often have a natural inclination to help others that draws them to the ministry initially. We hear Jesus' call to use our talents and respond with generosity, giving ourselves to his service. We often have an intuitive sense of how to help others, or what they can do to help themselves, which is a great gift.

But in spiritual direction, our job is different than parent, teacher, boss, politician, or therapist. Spiritual directors don't meet with another to tell that person how to live or solve personal problems.

Rather, our primary job as spiritual director is to help a directee discover their deepest desires in prayer, and then direct that person to God. In this way, a spiritual director allows the directee to discover the desires of the heart and allows God to give any solutions.

In his book, ***Allowing the Creator to Deal with the Creature,*** [4] William Barry, SJ writes, "One of my favorite questions for directees is the one Jesus put to the two disciples who began to follow him, 'What are you looking for?' (Jn 1:38) …. Nothing is more important for development of our relationship with God, for our prayer, in other words, than knowledge of what we want and of what God wants." But we as spiritual directors are not missioned with telling a person what to look for, of what God wants. No, this must come from within, during prayer. Our job as spiritual director is to facilitate this search for inner truth.

Be God's conduit instead of a guru.

Whether or not we realize or appreciate it, the training and prayerful wisdom create a power differential between spiritual director and directee. The title of "spiritual director" should remind those who use it of this power differential. A spiritual director has power, just by nature of the position. This means:
- Spiritual director must not abuse the power. Instead, you as spiritual director must work toward humility.
- A spiritual director's job is to direct people to God.
- A spiritual director has questions; answers are in the directee and God. Our job is to lead the directee there to find them.
- A spiritual director notices and comments so that the directee can see the reflection of God within.

One of my directees said, "I don't know how to stop telling my kids and everyone else what to do. I've been trained from infancy to be directive! I know how to fix stuff and clean stuff and it drives me nuts when people (especially my kids) act in stupid ways, or don't clean up! That's why I'm bossy." She is not alone in this. We have all been taught to find solutions and give them. From infancy on, we have been told how to act, so certainly we know how to direct others.

When you give God space to act, you as spiritual director help the directee to notice God acting. Congratulations! You are doing your job as spiritual director. The more you learn to refrain from problem-solving or instruction, the greater freedom you will have to let God to work in your directee, and the less you will be seen as a guru, teacher, or person with answers.

In both spiritual direction and supervision, you as spiritual director and supervisee must learn a new way of acting. Let your supervisory group help you learn how to trust God more so that you aren't tempted to provide solutions, even when asked. Learn to trust your supervisory group members so you open yourself to inspection in supervision. Learn to let God provide solutions beyond your understanding for both you and your directee.

Giving God freedom and letting go of control will deepen your freedom to explore places of interest, concern, understanding, or confusion in yourself, and thus deepen your relationship with God. Supervision helps us remain humble and keeps us focused on being the best director possible.

How to get out of God's way

To begin directing toward God, minimize or even eliminate instructions, examples, or teaching to your directee. When a directee mentions an issue that you think you've got an answer for, stop and pray; don't jump in with a solution. Then, 1)

Invite your directee to pray for help and ask God what to say next. 2) Remind your directee to trust God, 3) Help the directee to notice where God is acting. 4) Ask for his or her opinion. If your directee responds, "I don't know," answer, "Take a guess!"

Goals for Supervision include:

- Increase inner freedom, transparency and humility.
- Practice honesty in presenting and listening.
- Enlighten, energize, and elevate each member of the supervision group.
- Improve spiritual direction skills such as self-awareness and listening.
- Open the heart and soul more fully to God so both director and directee grow more God-centered.
- Improve ability to concentrate on the movements happening within the directee.
- Develop close relationships, trust, and respect among members.

Types of Supervision

Supervision can be performed in at least two different ways: individually with a supervisor and spiritual director one-on-one, or it can be performed with a group of spiritual directors who supervise one another.

Individual Supervision

With the individual supervision, a person trained in supervision meets individually with a spiritual director to supervise him or her one to one. This usually has a cost since the time and education of the supervisor is valuable and can even be the supervisor's livelihood.

Peer Supervision

In the second type of supervision, a group of spiritual directors meet regularly to supervise each other. The group must have at least one person trained in supervision for spiritual directors who can ensure the integrity of the group, keeping it focused. This type of supervision provides much more supervision experience for you as spiritual director, especially if you are directing just one or two people at a time.

When supervision is done in a group setting, with more than one supervisory member, and when spiritual directors know each other and meet as community for supervision, each spiritual director can hear what others are saying and experiencing. The ideal number for such a group is variable, but usually 3-4 people works best. All our interns who participate in group supervision express gratitude for what they hear and learn from others during supervision of another spiritual director. They each learn what to pay attention to and what to listen for by hearing what the others say in supervision. Everyone benefits from this process. Supervision expands your experience and wisdom.

Here are just a few of the many ways you will benefit from participating in group supervision.
- Learn from others' experiences.
- Expand understanding of the supervision process.
- Realize each person has something to give others.
- Grow in humility and appreciate humiliation.
- Improve listening and observational skills.
- Improve self-evaluation skills.
- Deepen the focus on affectivity.
- Expand appreciation of the Body of Christ, of prayer, and of spiritual direction.

Lead Supervisor

Because the supervision process is neither easy nor intuitive, when you form a group of spiritual directors for supervision, your group will need a lead supervisor to guide the group. This person must be a trained as a supervisor with a few years' experience in the craft, or someone who has been in supervision for several years. Such a person can help the group stay focused on the mission and core values so that the session rightly focuses on the spiritual director rather than the directee. A lead supervisor helps maintain integrity of the group and meet the needs of the members.

This book will focus on techniques and methods for group supervision so that you can develop experience in the spiritual life and deepen your ability to help lead souls to Christ.

Questions

1. Why do I feel called to be a spiritual director?
2. What is my reaction to the word "director" and what do I think about directing a person toward God?
3. What is my initial reaction to supervision? Why?
4. What attracts me about supervision? What repels me?
5. What do I think God is calling me to in relation to supervision?

1 Confidentiality

At its best, peer supervision provides several benefits including:
1) an opportunity for director growth,
2) better direction for directees, and
3) deeper understanding of the process for all participants. During supervision, peer group members and presenter mutually discern the presenter's spiritual movements that either block or facilitate his/her directee's prayer life.

In this intimate situation, peers must always respect the tension between their own curiosity and the boundaries of confidentiality. The format and suggestions provided in this book are meant to help spiritual directors stay within the boundaries of confidentiality and make sure the private lives of those we serve are not exposed unnecessarily. This can be especially difficult in smaller communities, where those who direct may know those who are being directed. Thus, it is very helpful to practice confidentiality during supervision.

To ensure that our supervision groups act ethically, we need to understand what ethical conduct looks like in relation to spiritual direction and supervision.

As a definition, ethical conduct is a manner of acting and speaking that flows from reverence for each person, including self. This reverence is shown through action and intention and extends into the spiritual direction relationship. Several guidelines can give you a clearer picture of how to stay ethical and assist other spiritual directors in your supervisory group to pursue integrity, responsibility, and faithfulness in their ministry and provide a God-centered service of others.

Confidentiality in Supervision

Let's start with the confidentiality within your peer group during supervision. Clarify for the directee what your process for evaluating the relationship is, including supervision.

To be clear, supervision is confidential. Always. Every part of supervision is confidential. Assume supervision to have the same seal as that of a priest concerning confession.

It is your job as group member, either as supervisor or presenter, to keep what is said in the supervision session in the confines of the group and the session. That means you don't discuss any part of the supervision session after the session is over unless necessary for training or continued supervision. Just don't speak of it outside of the supervision session.

Tell no "juicy" stories heard in supervision, even anonymously, to anyone. Set aside your curiosity; refuse to give solutions or "fix" a situation, consider everything you hear in supervision to be gossip outside of supervision. In other words, keep it all to yourself.

Stay focused on the presenter. Say as little as possible about the directee and focus on your reaction or experience. At your first spiritual direction session, inform your directee that you will be supervised. Assure the directee that you will not share confidential information with others unless you ask permission first. Then keep your word.

In your retreat community, tension can occur while trying to decide what is public and what is confidential information. To be safe, say nothing about your directee to anyone.

In speech and in your supervision papers, eliminate unnecessary details that might connect the subject of your supervision to your specific directee. This can be delicate and complicated in smaller groups, where each director may have only one directee. But if everyone in the group focuses on confidentiality, it is possible to compartmentalize the situation and the details in your brain, and not connect them to any person outside of the supervision session. This is what you should do every time you participate in supervision.

Instead of focusing on the directee, discuss *your* thoughts, feelings, responses, or reactions. You might imagine the verbatim conversation to be like the scaffolding on which you build the story of your own feelings, needs, and any desires that occurred IN YOU (your affect) during the spiritual direction session. This is one of the hardest aspects of supervision to understand and to follow. It is human nature to talk about the issues we encounter with a directee. We want to ferret out why this person doesn't pray enough, or doesn't act as we do, or what we can do to help the presenting director solve a directee's problems.

But during supervision, what the directee does or says is never the focus. Rather, the focus should be, and must stay on the director who is being supervised. The job of every member of the peer group, then, is to remember this, and bring the conversation back to the presenter every single time the conversation strays. This is vitally important. If you do this, your supervision sessions will accomplish the goal for which they are intended – helping the spiritual director deepen self-awareness.

In his article, "Supervision Improves Ministry", William Barry SJ, PhD, writes, "It would not surprise me to discover that the persistent temptation in individual and group supervision to concentrate on the absent person or persons (namely the clients or directees) stems from the reluctance to fact such self-revelations through real supervision. Yet directors know how much they admire directees who honestly face their weaknesses and limitations and sinfulness before the Lord and know too that such honest confrontation is the royal road to consolation.... They only way of becoming a more helpful director is through the challenge of honest self-evaluation."[5]

Be truthful and accurate. Write the verbatim conversation as it occurred. The team needs to hear what you said in response to what your retreatant said. Your responses and affect are the most important, since you are the person being supervised. So, while you are being truthful and accurate, ensure that your presentation stays confidential. To do this, summarize or generalize any confidential aspects of the conversation. For instance, a directee says something like, "I just realized I'm addicted to alcohol. I drink too much and here's how it affects my prayer..." Your verbatim can summarize and simply write, "I have just realized I have a serious attachment. Here's how it has affected my prayer..."

Refrain from defining the nature of any personal struggle shared by a directee unless that is relevant to your response. If a person tells you of an argument between himself and his wife concerning money, for instance, you can quote the directee as saying: "I had a struggle with my spouse about a serious issue."

Refrain from mentioning confidential material either within supervision or outside of it. If you feel called to discuss something about your directee that seems too personal for the supervision group to know or hear about, talk to an individual supervisor, your spiritual director, your program director, or another mentor about the issue. Together both of you can discern if you should bring up the situation to the group in supervision. Otherwise, as mentioned before, speaking about any part of supervision outside of the supervision session is akin to gossip. In an interview, Pope Francis said, "Gossip destroys coexistence, the family. It is a hidden disease. It is the plague." [6] See **When to Break Confidentiality** below for more details on this.

Always use pseudonyms – Don't use initials or the actual name for your directee, especially if others know who you are directing. Your job is to make your directee as anonymous as possible. When you give the background information for this person, include details that focus on the spiritual life. Add information such as age, marital status, children, or occupation only if necessary for the group to understand the conversation. Here are a few examples:

- Susan prays for 30 minutes each day on most days. I notice her increased awareness of God's presence.
- Maria is a middle-aged woman hoping to discover the 'magis' (more) of God. She is patient, trusting that God will provide, but unable to recognize her feelings without help.
- Lancelot wants to deepen his relationship with God and find a wife. He says he wants to learn how to hear what God is telling him and learn discernment so he can decide well.

If you avoid more specific life details such as number of children, spouse, age, marital status, etc., it makes confidentiality easier. As you write the description of your directee, ask yourself, "Is this aspect about my directee's life relevant to this supervision session?" If so, include it. If not, exclude it.

Other Important Considerations for Confidentiality

Besides verbal confidentiality, it's also important to keep confidential all oral, electronic, and written matters arising in the spiritual direction or supervision sessions. Make sure your notes are not left in a place where others might access them. Recognize and disclose to the spiritual directee the limitations of confidentiality of electronic communications. Finally, conduct spiritual direction and supervision sessions in appropriate, private settings. This means you don't meet in the coffee shop, restaurant, or library unless there's a private room for your use. If you meet in a home, make sure it's private but not intimate.

Don't stop educating yourself.

It is important for you as spiritual director to engage in ongoing formation and continuing education. Consider spiritual direction as your calling, requiring on-going growth to serve your directees well.

No one knows everything, even if you've attended the best program, got an advanced degree, was ordained, or have thirty years' experience, there is always more to learn. Plus, spiritual direction is relational. That means, depending on who you are directing, the relationship between you and your directee will generate new issues, theories, values, and ideas. Culture, the church, and your other relationships will contribute to what goes on within you to enhance, diminish, or even negate truth. Things you learned in the past can be forgotten.

Your mission as a spiritual director and member of the supervisory peer group is to stay engaged and informed. Make a plan that outlines how you can deepen and expand your insight into the ways in which culture, society, history, environment, and how institutions impact your world view. You can use prayer, study, and supervision to do so.

Topics for continuing education that you might need to focus on include sacred scripture, theology, spirituality, psychology, communication techniques, and other disciplines related to spiritual direction. Read within and outside of your comfort zone, so you understand other voices and opinions that might not harmonize with yours.

Balance spiritual direction with other aspects of life.

Each person takes on multiple roles and has many relationships that take time and attention. Evaluate your schedule often to ensure you are not overworked or stretched too thin.

Make time for daily prayer, work, leisure, family, and personal relationships. Spiritual direction can't be just one more activity or ministry that you perform along with many others. It requires a commitment of your time and energy. Spiritual direction is much bigger than just sitting with a retreatant once a week. Beyond meeting with a directee, you will need to allot time in your schedule for much more, including direction session preparation, direction session recording, writing the supervision paper, attending supervision, continuing your spiritual direction and supervision skill education, developing your listening skills, values, and emotions; and most importantly, practicing regular daily prayer. It's best if you err on the side of doing less than doing more outside of your spiritual direction commitment.

Here are some things you can do to help keep your life in balance while continuing to serve Christ as a spiritual director.

- Accept the truth that supervision is not 'extra' beyond spiritual direction. It is part of the process. Thus, you must plan it into your life and schedule time for supervision just as you schedule meetings with directees in spiritual direction.
- Schedule appropriate space between meetings and directees.
- Continue regular education including retreats, conferences and reading on spiritual direction and supervision.
- St. Ignatius said that discernment takes at least two people and prayer. Thus, before you decide to add any more directees, tasks, ministries, or activities to your schedule, pray first, then talk to your personal spiritual director, a trusted friend or family member, your supervisory peer group, or your superior about your decision. You will be able to say no or yes with confidence when you know what God calls you to do.

Listen to God and supervisors about who you direct.

Spiritual directors are called to honor the dignity of the spiritual directee. You as spiritual director need to respect the spiritual directee's values, culture, conscience, and spirituality. This is not always easy, especially if you encounter values or spirituality that are foreign to your experience or that you judge to conflict with God's values (Ten Commandments, beatitudes, church teachings).

If you are directing someone who expresses distinctly different values, culture, or spirituality than you do, prayerfully consider how you will address these issues. Ask yourself: "Can I listen without judgement to this person's story, even if it conflicts or opposes my own value system? Should I?"

We are not always called to direct a person that asks us for direction, or the person who comes to us through a program such as the Spiritual Exercises. If you have doubts about directing a particular person, prayerfully consider your call to do so. A while ago, my parish priest asked me to direct a woman who was addicted to pornography. On one hand, I felt glad that he had recognized the value of spiritual direction, and responsible to do as he asked. But on the other hand, I felt a bit overwhelmed and unprepared for a person with this problem. I had no experience with this issue. With prayer, I realized I was not the right person to direct her; I turned down the job.

Be Honest with Yourself

Perhaps you became a spiritual director because you have a loving heart and want to help people become the best they can be. Most likely you have been helping others your whole life. You enjoy watching God work in the world, especially in the lives of those you serve. So sometimes, it is difficult to say no. But fortunately, supervision allows us the opportunity to discuss thoughts about who to direct and why with others, so you aren't duping yourself into directing or not directing another.

Through supervision, you can assess value conflicts as they arise. If you are honest about your abilities, motivation, and conflicts, you will be able to say no (or yes) when called to do so.

If you continue with a difficult situation, stay aware of your response to the directee and take any feelings of anger, frustration, or disappointment that you experience regarding spiritual direction to your supervisory group. Do so to prevent such issues negatively affecting the spiritual direction session or your own mental, spiritual, or physical health.

In spiritual direction, you have a responsibility to God first and to your directee second. If you believe that either God or your supervisory peer group (or both) suggest that it's not appropriate for you to direct any person, trust their evaluation.

For example, Joan, a Christian spiritual director, was directing a young woman named Laura, who was living in a tumultuous marriage. They spent months on the rules for discernment and discussed the positive and negative attributes of the married life as well as staying single. Finally, Laura decided not to marry but instead live with her boyfriend. Joan was shocked and surprised.

In supervision Joan identified feelings of judgment and frustration. And she felt deep sorrow and disappointment in Laura's final choice. Her supervisors helped her realize that she was unable to remain neutral with Laura. Joan concluded that she could no longer continue as the spiritual director for Laura, who had chosen to live outside of her Biblical values. Joan decided to step back from the relationship. To her directee, she said, "I don't believe I am the best person to be directing you right now. I can assist you with finding a new spiritual director."

Beyond conflicts, it is important to remove yourself from any situation where the integrity of the spiritual direction relationship is compromised and where you are not unduly influenced by the directee. Step away from directing a person if:

- You feel threatened.
- You feel sexually attracted to the retreatant.
- You can't find a time when both of you can meet.
- You perceive that the situation will take more skill or effort than you have.

When to Break Confidentiality

You must break confidentiality if there is a legitimate concern of physical or psychological harm, or if the situation is life-threatening to the directee, to you the spiritual director, or to others. In such cases, you as director should tell your program director or supervisors, who will contact the appropriate authorities. If, for example, your directee says he or she is considering suicide or murder, or describes child or elder abuse, you should inform the directee of your concern, and let him or her know you'll be discussing the issue with persons of authority.

One of our spiritual directors was working with a directee who appeared to have a demonic oppression. Within supervision, the director decided to continue spiritual direction as long as the person entered therapy.

In the 35 years that I've been directing the Spiritual Exercises, I've encountered a few people with mental issues serious enough to impact spiritual direction. The circumstances of these were discussed in supervision and referred to therapy.

Although it's unlikely you will encounter any directees who are suicidal or threatening harm to another, it is possible. So be prepared. Know what your options are and how you will proceed should the need arise. Identify a few trusted therapists to whom you can refer any directee and have their contact information ready should you need it.

Summary

To provide the correct environment for supervision, you as a member of a supervisory peer group should be attending church services, praying daily, and meeting with your personal spiritual director regularly. These steps will fortify your spiritual growth and health, so you are stronger spiritually and emotionally for the job you are called to do.

Nurture your self-knowledge and freedom. This involves self-evaluation and education. To increase your self-knowledge, you can take courses, seminars, read books, read the Bible, and use the Ignatian Examen to get to know yourself and God more deeply. Take time daily to consider where your spirit feels freedom and where you harbor doubt, pride, or other issues that might impact your ability to listen or focus.

The more you can heal and eradicate issues that detract from or derail your focus on God, the freer you'll be to lead your directee to God. This is a never-ending process, but one that will enrich both you and your directee.

Spiritual direction is not just a job. It's a ministry where you as spiritual director give your whole self – mind, spirit, and body – to another person for a short period of time, so that you are in their service completely. This is what supervision is about and why you will do a much better job as spiritual director if you are regularly supervised yourself.

Questions

1. In what ways could I be more intentional in my confidentiality in relation to my record-keeping?
2. Where do I feel free to be myself? Where do I feel tied up?
3. How well do I keep confidential all that happens in spiritual direction and supervision? How can I improve on these?
4. What area of personal growth am I lacking, and where do I need to grow?

5. How can I begin to deepen my understanding and education in the areas I identified as lacking?
6. "How well do I feel capable of setting aside my beliefs, spirituality, or culture and truly listen to what my directee says?"

2 Two Standards for Supervision

"You cannot lead where you do not go."

In his Spiritual Exercises, St. Ignatius Loyola presents the Two Standards – a vision of reality in terms of two different value systems. In this system, Saint Ignatius' helps us clarify the difference between the value system of Christ and the value system of Evil.

Author Michael Ivens S.J. writes in **Understanding the Spiritual Exercises**, that St. Ignatius presents these two values systems "not in their obvious ways of working, but in their subtleties. Thus, the power of evil is shown as operating plausibly yet destructively, through the appeal of objectively legitimate **riches and honours**. And life in Christ is not just a morally correct life, but one that values the paradoxes of spiritual and actual poverty."[7]

One important word in that quote, "***plausibly***," helps us to understand why the study of the Two Standards and continual striving to follow the standard of Christ is vital for good supervision. People often feel justified and even righteous in action or making decisions based on the worldly standard. This worldly standard is ***plausible*** – meaning it is believable, credible, or comfortable. It's what our family, or schools, and our businesses teach us to pay attention to, to value, and to learn.

The Two Standards meditation takes those who pray through it to considerations focused on their negative and positive qualities. In this process, a person can more easily realize how personal desires, attitudes, and actions fit into one standard or the other.

St. Ignatius includes riches, honor, and pride into the Standard of Evil. The Standard of Christ includes poverty, humility, and humiliation.

The Standard of the World

*When one lives attached to money, pride or power, it is impossible to be truly happy. ~***Pope Francis**

St. Ignatius says that those who follow the Standard of Evil value riches, honor, and pride. Those who follow the Standard of Evil might believe they are seeking comfort, personal success, getting even, and avoiding pain at all costs. These actions promise self-satisfaction and seem so ***plausible***, and intuitive. They are almost comfortable. In this way, the Standard of Evil appeals to the ego.

We tell our children to study so they can get a good job with a decent salary when they grow up. The marketing department for Hollywood stars promote the Oscars, magazines about actors, fashion, and movie ads that all try to convince us that riches, honor, and pride are ***plausible*** goals for life. Social Media, movies, video games, and many cultural activities including sports promote the values of power and selfishness. Ads tell us to "get your own bag" of chips; don't share. The "good guy" protagonist is often violent, killing all who get in his way of vengeance. We are told we "deserve" nice hair or pretty skin because we are "worth it." On the other hand, gratitude for what we've been given is not important nor is it promoted. Being other-centered is considered wishy-washy or worse, weak.

But Evil (Otherwise known as Satan, falsity, the Enemy, Father of Lies) does not have our best interest at heart. Evil tries to destroy relationships between people, especially those working to follow Christ. Make no mistake, the goal of evil is complete slavery of the human heart. The usual weapons to accomplish this goal are fraud, lies and deceit, hidden agendas, and subterfuge and most especially, the ego. Living under the standard of Evil enslaves us. Here's how.

Riches - *(I want) can lead to greed, compulsion, and possessiveness.*

The word 'riches' refers to more than just money. Riches convey a sense of security and independence. In the case of supervision and spirituality, it's tempting to see wisdom or knowledge concerning the method or concepts, or spiritual depth as riches. Valued above God, any riches, including spiritual, can lead us to the Evil Standard.

The Standard of the World has been culturally ingrained into most people's hearts and minds from childhood. It makes worldly sense. Culture tells us that riches are the way to happiness. Michael Ivens writes, "Taken literally, riches and honor refer to material possessions, and social and ecclesiastical status, but while this literal sense has relevance for everyone in every age (and crucial implications for our own age), the terms also admit of wider application. In the wider sense, ***riches and honor*** can be anything at all that meets the inherent human need for identity, security, esteem, love."[8] Riches prompt a person toward desire and greed. Focusing on riches fosters compulsions and possessiveness, and as a result, squeezes God out of our lives.

In Mark 10: Jesus tells the rich young man to "go, sell all you have and follow me." He couldn't do that so he walked away sad. If we choose riches over Christ, we too will walk away sad from Jesus' message.

Of course, wealth and riches are not evil in themselves. All that God created is good. It is in the desire for riches, and the disordered attachment to them that Satan uses to tempt and trap us, and in the end, enslave us.

Honor - (I deserve) makes me more important than God.

Our culture communicates the World's standard. Schools often teach and promote self-esteem above self-respect and self-control. Movies, books, and other media promote ego. Violence is seen as the response to dishonor. Even children's cartoons show the protagonist using force to champion wrongs. Honor becomes the goal for every action. The honor-seeker is constantly aware of others, and asks, "What do others think of me? How can I get more attention, more notoriety, and more honor? What do I need to wear, look like, do, or say to be honored?"

This seeking affirmation and confirmation from others develops a skewed sense of "justice." Here's how it works. People who hunger for honor insist others "respect" them (the meaning of respect is defined by the one seeking honor, of course.) When a perceived "disrespect" occurs, the honor-seeker easily resorts to anger, or revenge, and demanding that others atone for perceived insults or slights. Honor seekers feel justified in posting insults on social media, or telling friends, neighbors, and others. In their mind, this is "just," since the perceived offense diminished their honor. God's values are not part of the equation.

Pride - (I own – this is MINE!) tricks me into believing that I am self-sufficient, and I need nothing and no one else, not even God.

According to Michael Ivans, pride is a "stance in relation to God, consisting in the refusal to give praise and reverence, and hence a tendency, in however subtle a way, to try to establish oneself as absolute." [9] Pride whispers "*I am very important, more important than you. I deserve to have what I want, and you must give it to me.*"

We first hear about pride in Genesis 3 of the Bible as the serpent uses pride to tempt Adam and Eve to disobey God. Since then, pride has spread to every person in the world.

St. Ignatius Loyola listed pride as the root of all evil. In the chapter on pride in **Mere Christianity** Author C.S. Lewis wrote, "According to Christian teachers, the essential vice, the utmost evil, is Pride. Unchastity, anger, greed, drunkenness, and all that, are mere flea bites in comparison: it was through Pride that the devil became the devil. Pride leads to every other vice: it is the complete anti-God state of mind… it is Pride which has been the chief cause of misery in every nation and every family since the world began."[10]

According to the world's standard, you should not love enemies as Jesus tells us to do, but instead hate those who hate you. Blame others for your problems, wield power over them when possible, and insist that others change to make you comfortable. This helps keep us strong and proud, our culture tells us.

Following the World's Standard, we don't give glory to God for talents or abilities. Instead, we pride ourselves for personal accomplishments, and God becomes irrelevant. Proud persons don't need to discover who God created them to be, but instead embrace the cultural lie that we can be anything we WANT to be. And in this wanting, desire becomes god, and pride pushes us forward to seek the desire.

On the flip side, we are trained to keep vulnerabilities and emotions hidden (especially negative or counter-cultural ones) or we are encouraged to weaponize them to control others. This helps maintain the charade that we are somehow perfect or better than others.

The Standard of Christ

The Standard of Christ is opposite the Evil standard; it is counter cultural. Few people, even most followers of Christ, believe that poverty, humility, and humiliation are blessings. Yet, the spiritual director is asked to embrace humility and humiliation with fervor because we must live what we teach.

Christ's Standard tells us to value the poor in spirit, the meek, those who hunger and thirst for righteousness, the merciful, the peacemakers, and those persecuted for the cause of right. None of this is easy, and none of these values are promoted in our culture. But as we embrace Jesus' standard and value system, we gain freedom. We no longer are at the whim of our feelings. Instead, we are truthful about our affectivity, about the emotions we feel, and attribute our feelings to our values and needs, and we follow Christ's standard more fully. When a friend turns me down for a favor, I choose not to feel slighted, following a value of self. Instead, I choose to value my friend's needs. When the weather turns gray, I can be thankful for God's gift of life. (more on this in Chapter 5)

Saint Paul, in his letter to the Colossians wrote: "Put on, as God's chosen ones, holy and beloved, compassion, kindness, humility, meekness, and patience, bearing with one another and forgiving one another if one has a grievance against another; as the Lord has forgiven you, so must you also do. And over all these put on love, that is, the bond of perfection. And let the peace of Christ control your hearts, the peace into which you were also called in one Body."[11]

Every person who enters spiritual direction and supervision must 'put on Christ' in this way. This will ensure that spiritual direction and supervision are done well.

St. Ignatius lists three degrees of humility. The third degree of humility, Ignatius described as, "most perfect humility; namely, when – including the first and second and the praise and glory of the Divine Majesty being equal – in order to imitate and be more actually like Christ our Lord, I want to choose poverty with Christ poor rather than riches, contempt with Christ replete with it rather than honors; and to desire to be rated as worthless and a fool for Christ, who first was held as such, rather than wise or prudent in this world."[12]

Let's look at each aspect of Christ's standard to see how they can bring freedom into supervision.

Poverty – I am generous, I enjoy giving and serving.

Following Christ's standard leads to poverty, a realization that all things are gifts from God. Those who follow Christ's standard don't let wealth dictate who they are. They are generous with what they have so others can live a better life.

Practicing poverty in relation to supervision means you share knowledge or wisdom with humility. You realize that no one has all the answers except God. You admit that each person in your group, even the newest member, has unique ideas and gifts that could provide insight for any circumstance.

Michael Ivens, S.J. defines spiritual poverty as "an attitude that does not look to riches and honour for a security cover against God, but which uses and enjoys these gifts, and only in relation to God's service and praise. Spiritual poverty does not necessarily imply actual poverty, but it does imply openness to it. Where *actual poverty* in any form is simply unacceptable, a non-value, there is no spiritual poverty."[13] Poverty promotes generosity. It brings enjoyment in service.

Those who give to others generously deepen the gifts of gratitude and selflessness in return. There's a deep joy in helping and giving to others that is fostered in the attitude of poverty.

Humility – I am loved by God, I am a child of God.

As we know, in every spiritual direction session, God (not you or me) is the spiritual director. That means, as you stand in for God as spiritual director, you must learn to release the ego and let the creator deal directly with the creature. The more you depend on God for every part of the experience, the easier spiritual direction becomes.

Humility deepens dependency on God. When you embrace humility in spiritual direction and in supervision, you can more easily and humbly point to the true Spiritual Director, God Almighty. God calls us to release personal desires and goals, even in spiritual direction, such as "helping" or "leading to a desired outcome." Instead, we embrace the truth that we are imperfect, cracked or even broken earthen vessels. This frees us for discernment and obedience, and along with that, humility, humiliation and poverty.

Humility lets me recognize that I am a child of God, I am loved for who I am, just as I am. I can let God free my ego and my desire to look good and instead embrace authenticity. A directee does not need the spiritual director to be perfect. Instead, every directee needs his or her spiritual director to be humble and open to the Holy Spirit so God can do the work through them. Humility deepens your understanding and appreciation of gentleness, honesty, receptivity.

Humiliation and Insults – I am comfortable in my identity and good because God made me.

When we embrace humiliation and even insults for the sake of the Gospel, we develop the virtues of powerlessness and encouragement. Jesus said, "Blessed are those who are persecuted for the sake of righteousness, for theirs is the kingdom of heaven."

I'm not saying you should seek out persecution, nor that you as supervisor should inflict it. But supervision is a challenging process that can be uncomfortable at times. We all want to look good in the eyes of others, so telling the truth about self isn't always pretty. You might be asked to look at aspects of yourself that you don't want to address or are ashamed of, such as prior attachments, ways in which you avoid candor, how you deal with uncomfortable issues, etc. Supervisors don't intend to bring such a response, but you might feel persecuted or even insulted during supervision. If so, pray that you can learn and grow from this humiliation, and embrace it as Christ-like suffering. If you see this as a way in which you grow to become less self-protective, and more Christ-like, then you are using it to bring you closer to Christ.

As mentioned above, you might think embracing humiliation makes you too vulnerable or exposed. It's easy to worry that you will be judged harshly. You might ask yourself, "What will the others think of me if I reveal my error, poor judgement, inattention, my overblown response, or any of the myriad other issues that could arise during supervision. Can I trust them?"

The question then becomes, trust them for what? Don't trust that the group will protect your ego or keep you from dealing with difficult subjects. Don't trust that your group will be 'nice' and never challenge you or your motives. Instead, you can trust that the team will try to help you expose parts of your inner self that interfere with the spiritual growth of you or your directee. You can trust that God will be with you in the moment of exposure and will make sure you are given the grace to make it through. You can trust that your group wants what's best for you and your directee and will help you discover it.

If any inquiry gets too intense for you, say so. You should tell the group that you are overwhelmed and that the questions are too much for you. Then allow the group to help you uncover why, within yourself, you judge the conversation to be too intense.

Fruits of the Spirit

The Catechism of the Catholic Church [1832] tells us that, "The *fruits* of the Spirit are perfections that the Holy Spirit forms in us as the first fruits of eternal glory. The tradition of the Church lists twelve of them: 'charity, joy, peace, patience, kindness, goodness, generosity, gentleness, faithfulness, modesty, self-control, and chastity.'"[14] These fruits are necessary for Christ-centered spiritual direction and spiritual supervision.

As you and your supervision partners deepen your love for Christ, you will hone your ability to follow Christ's Standard as you practice poverty, humility, and humiliation. The fruits of this spiritual conversion will begin to grow in your life and in your supervision sessions.

Developing these fruits provides a clear indication that you are accomplishing supervision according to Christ's Standard and they will transform you and members of your group. So, take time after every meeting to evaluate which fruits you've seen in the session, and celebrate them. With practice and awareness, you as spiritual director will begin to recognize and develop the fruits that grow from following Christ's standard. And you'll then increase your ability to help directees develop those fruits.

Summary

The Ignatian Spirituality Two Standards meditation becomes important, not just for the directee, but also for the spiritual director preparing for supervision. The Two Standards are also vital for the supervisory group members to study and practice as they prepare to supervise.

When you embrace and practice the values found in Jesus' Standard - poverty, humility, and humiliation - you will begin to see growth of the fruits of the Spirit in your life, in your spiritual direction, and in your supervision sessions. Watch for an increase of receptivity, selflessness, love, powerlessness, generosity, gentleness, honesty, gratefulness, and encouragement. These fruits, which might seem unattractive culturally, are vital for spiritual growth. And they are signs of Christ and his Standard in the world.

Those who follow Christ's Standard know that a person's feelings don't depend on others' actions, the weather, or circumstances. Each person generates his or her own feelings from his or her own personal values and standards.

When you trust that every feeling you have is generated from a value you hold that is either affirmed, weakened, or quashed, you will act and be differently. You will gain control over your feelings and be able to change them by recognizing and changing the values that drive them. You can decide to be happy or sad because when you change a value, the feelings change with it.

Questions

1. If I truly believe that Jesus loves me and wants to save me from evil, how can I embrace mercy, meekness, and accepting persecution for what is right more fully?
2. What does it look like for me to set myself aside to follow Christ's Standard and embrace poverty of spirit, humility, and other-centeredness?
3. How can I, as supervisory group member, help the group stay focused on Christ's Standard?
4. What aspects of poverty, humility and humiliation are toughest for me to incorporate into my life and spiritual direction sessions? What can I do to promote those aspects in my life and direction sessions?

3 Worldly Model Expanded

In his book, Sacred Fire, author Ronald Rolheiser writes, "Anthropologists tell us that, until we can create community with each other at a certain level, that is on the basis of what we positively and mutually stand for, we create community with each by its opposite, by what we are mutually against."[15] This is a model that any supervision group can easily fall into, but a model that is not conducive to good supervision.

Let's explore what a supervision community would look like and how members might act should they follow a Worldly Model or cultural meeting dynamic.

If the supervision process follows the Worldly Model like supervision or meeting with superiors in the workplace, the process might feel like a test or an inquisition.

- Participants often enter the supervision process with trepidation, fearing others' judgement.
- Participants feel nervous that they might say something "wrong" and feel anxious about being chastised for it.
- Group members think it is acceptable for actions and conversations to be criticized or even invalidated.
- At the end of the process of supervision, the presenter might see the process as ineffective, placating, useless, or even threatening.
- Groups who practice this model become either too stressful or a waste of time and eventually fall apart.

I'll use an example of a spiritual director named Monique throughout this section to help illustrate how to recognize the Worldly Model.

Help and Support

Each group member tries to protect his or her own self-image or self-esteem above everything. When it is helpful to keep the peace, to help the person supervised feel comfortable, to make sure the person returns next time, or for a member to look magnanimous, supervision group participants act "nice" and give approval and praise. Negative feelings are minimized, and the group focuses on positive feelings. This might prevent the supervised person from feeling badly, but also prevents deeper introspection into negative affectivity. This also promotes peace at the price of honesty.

At other times, a peer member might be over-directive and manipulative, and want to ensure that the presenter and others behave 'properly' according to their own idea of what that means. Peers then become judgmental and look for ways to correct the presenter. The focus is on correct actions and conversations. Sometimes this might be how a peer normally acts. Sometimes a peer is worried about losing power or prestige and so denigrates the presenter to keep him or her in line.

Alternately, a peer group member may feel over-protective of the presenter or another peer. In this case, the group member might run interference and prevent others from asking deeper questions, or shame, blame, or belittle the peer to stop the direction of the conversation. This is usually done in the name or protection, where the interrupting person believes that the presenter can't stand up for him- or herself.

Monique arrived at the supervision meeting late. She had gotten to bed late and overslept in the morning, so she took no time to pray or send her paper to everyone beforehand. Monique felt guilty and disappointed in herself, but also rebellious. She didn't like having to participate in supervision, nor did she trust the group members. She didn't mention that she hated supervision and was late mostly because she was trying to find a way to escape it. Instead, she mumbled an apology and sat down.

No one asked Monique why she didn't send the paper, or why she was late, or how she might evaluate her own attitude about supervision. Instead, the facilitator said, "You know our rule is that you send the paper to everyone beforehand. This time we will let it slide, but you must do this next time or we won't supervise you." One of the more compassionate peers, Becca, said, "I'm sure she didn't do this on purpose. I don't think we should belabor the point, Logan. Let's just forget this happened and move on."

Respect for others

In the worldly model, participants defer to others who have more seniority or stronger opinions and don't confront faulty reasoning or actions.

Thinking that it is helpful, the group members might avoid or minimize negative emotions and affect and focus on the positive only. Or they might focus only on the negative and keep the presenter on edge through what might feel like an interrogation. Peers may believe that over-sensitive, concerned interference is the same as respect, and try to protect the presenter from having to feel and explore emotions.

Rather than listen to what God is saying, or what the presenter says, participants presume they understand the presenter's circumstance and motives, or even emotions and then question or teach based on that presumption.

Monique was feeling nervous about judgement because at her last supervision session, she was interrogated about some of her actions. Following the supervision paper outline, Monique mentioned her stress and worry. "My thoughts wandered to the fight I had with my husband the night before. I think I ruined the directee's experience."

Logan, the most senior member of the group, picked up on her nervousness, rather than ask about it, he patted her hand and said, "I can see you are a person who is easily distracted. All spiritual directors struggle with that." Then he gave consultation without naming it as such and did not explore her emotions first. "Next time just ignore the fact that you got distracted and return to the conversation."

Ana felt patronized. She knew from other supervision sessions that the more experienced directors seemed to know how to focus better during their spiritual direction sessions. "Maybe he can read me, knows that I hate this, and is just trying to keep me from quitting," she thought.

No member of the peer group contradicted Logan, and no one pointed out that he had slipped into consultation or that he switched focus to the directee. Logan had most seniority and they didn't want to endure any verbal "correction" from their resident "guru."

Strength

Strength comes through power and position in the Worldly Model group, and the most knowledgeable, strongest or most verbal person speaks first. Vulnerability, humility, and humiliation are seen as weaknesses that are to be avoided. Issues are not evaluated in the light of truth and grace. They are considered self-explanatory. "Truth" is obvious (defined as what the group leaders promote). So, there is no need to explain or define reasoning. Those in power believe they have the "right" answer and hold their position to "win" power, compliments, feeling superior, or accomplishment.

Monique found it difficult to continue with the session. It didn't seem at all helpful to her, but she pressed on because this was what she promised to do while directing, and she was irritated that Logan assumed he knew how she felt. She didn't want to talk about any more feelings because she judged that the group would make assumptions about them, too. She felt invisible and the circumstance felt hopeless.

"I am easily distracted and thanks for the advice," Monique said.

Logan said, "Don't worry. You'll get this," he said. Then he reiterated, *"Just remember: ignore the fact that you got distracted and return to the conversation."*

Fear

In the Worldly Model, participants fear being wrong. A supervisory team member might feel compelled to remain silent during a supervision session to prevent embarrassment, fear of failure, fear of ridicule, or concern that any questions he or she want to ask might not be "right" according to the peer group members. Participants and presenters alike feel the pressure of fear. They don't always know the unspoken 'rules' for what is acceptable to say and what is not. So, it's often easier to say nothing and avoid any possibility of embarrassment. Group members are out to look good, not help the others in the group. They don't ask each other for opinions, and don't give the quieter members an opportunity to share or express their thoughts or affect.

Two of Monique's peers joined in the conversation by reiterating that she was doing just fine, and that distractions are nothing to be ashamed of. "Logan is right," one said, and congratulated Monique for bringing the issue to supervision. The other three members were silent, but no one asked them if they wanted to add anything. Everyone ignored Monique's written affectivity and the other issues she brought to supervision.

Monique felt confused by the discord between her own feelings and what the group was saying. She wasn't 'doing fine' in her own eyes and wished she could get some clearer picture of how to help make spiritual direction better and easier. But she felt uncomfortable about contradicting the others. Her fear of failure took over and she felt vulnerable and unheard. She didn't have the emotional energy to do anything else.

Honesty

Peers might feel compelled to tell others what they feel or think, regardless of how their thoughts or feelings affect the spiritual director or supervision session. Alternately, peers might distort or cover up truth in the interest of protecting others from hurt.

Logan said, "As far as distractions go, I think you are doing a good job in spiritual direction, Monique. You'll get better over time. I recall back when I first started, it took me a few years to really focus on the conversation. [He talked a while about his early years.] *My advice is to keep trying like you are doing."*

Monique felt confused by his advice. She didn't know exactly how to follow it and 'keep trying'. Logan didn't show her by role-playing how she should proceed. The others in the group just nodded agreement so Monique got no help from the other team members. She really wanted to talk about her distress and confusion, and her aversion to supervision in general, but she decided it wouldn't make any difference. No one seemed to be listening.

Integrity

In relation to integrity, those acting in the worldly model could go one of two ways during a supervision session. These include:

1. Suppress knowledge completely and focus only on feelings, or;
2. Focus only on principles, values, and beliefs and skip feelings, making peer supervisors sound very reasonable and knowledgeable.

Either way, the supervision session misses the focus on God, and what is happening within the presenter's heart and soul.

Throughout the supervision session, none of the peers asked Monique about her body language, her feelings or what her values and needs were that prompted any feeling. Instead, they discussed general principles and values. "You just need to look at your lack of attention in terms of time," one peer supervisor said, "It is difficult to fit spiritual direction into a busy life. You need to evaluate how well you are doing that!"

Another peer gave advice about how to manage life to make 'more time' for important things like meeting a directee. The conversation felt reasonable and logical. No one asked where she saw God in the struggle, or in the session, or what she felt called to do as far as time management went.

"The less I say, the better," Monique thought. "I don't seem to be on the same page as this group."

At the end of the supervision session, Monique felt demoralized. To her, the session hindered more than helped her growth and understanding of herself and of spiritual direction. Her gaze stayed on her hands and supervision paper rather than on her peer group members. She hoped to hide her anxiety and stress and felt glad now that she didn't have to explain her discomfort or her perceived failure. "I don't trust any of them with my feelings," she thought. "They all have their own interpretations; they don't need mine."

Worldly-Centered Model Summary

In summary, a worldly centered model takes a group from a focus on the whole person and God's interaction with the spiritual director and directee session, to a self-centered protectionist, formulaic method that keeps the status quo and prevents real personal interaction and growth.

Questions

1. Do you recognize any of the world-centered model attributes in your supervision meetings?
2. What aspect of the worldly model seems like the most harmful to your own experience in supervision? Why?
3. What values do I need to develop to help me stay out of the Worldly Model of supervision?

4 Christ-Centered Model Expanded

In ***The Holy Longing,*** Ronald Rolheiser mentions "four things as an essential praxis for a healthy spiritual life: a) private prayer and private morality, b) social justice, c) mellowness of heart and spirit; and d) community as a constitutive element of true worship."[16]

> **Let me have too deep a sense of humor ever to be proud. Let me know my absurdity before I act absurdly. Let me realize that when I am humble, I am most human, most truthful, and most worthy of your serious consideration.**
>
> —Daniel A. Lord, SJ, in ***Hearts on Fire: Praying with Jesuits***[17]

For effective supervision, you, as a member of a supervision group are called to develop mellowness of heart and spirit as well as community by focusing on and practicing the Christ-Centered Model Values in supervision and in all of life.

As we have learned above, in the Christ-Centered Model, God's Spirit brings to light what is hidden so that the spiritual director who is presenting can make free, co-creative choices which lead to graced and lasting relationships with God, the directee, and the supervisory group members. Following a Christ-centered model allows God's Spirit to enlighten your heart and mind. You'll soften by gratitude and openness.

When a group tries to follow the Christ-centered model for supervision, all peer group members benefit. Presenters recognize the freedom gained from following Christ. Peers feel free to explore attitudes, affectivity, and actions. Let's go through a supervision session with Monique again, this time we will follow the Christ-Centered Model.

Help and Support

In the Christ-centered model, peer supervision group members increase the others' capacity to engage and confront their own ideas. They assist in recognizing and identifying unsurfaced assumptions, biases, and fears. This is best done by revealing your own assumptions, fears, and biases to others. Be transparent and help those in your group to risk the same.

Protective peer group members realize that asking about feelings, affectivity, and the values, needs and standards from which those feelings grow is the foundation of supervision. Therefore, they don't allow any 'parental protection mode' to take over. Instead, they ask deeper questions and allow or encourage others to do so also. They prayerfully avoid any shame, blame, or belittling.

Monique arrived at the supervision meeting late. She had a late night and overslept, so she had no time to pray ahead of time. She didn't send her paper in and was unprepared for the session. Monique felt guilty and disappointed in herself, but also rebellious. She didn't like having to do supervision and didn't know the group members well. Instead of telling the others that, she mumbled an apology.

The facilitator, Sarah, said, "You look stressed, Monique. What's going on inside of you right now?"

Monique felt put on the spot, but also glad to talk about her distress. "I feel nervous about this. I don't like being judged and this feels a bit like that. Supervision is not my favorite thing to do."

"Can you identify what value that feeling of nervousness and not wanting to be judged is coming from, within you?" Sarah asked. "Take a minute to reflect. We want to help you explore that more deeply."

Respect for Others

Attribute to other people the ability for self-reflection and self-examination. Trust that they can see themselves without becoming so upset that they lose their effectiveness and their sense of self, responsibility, or choice. Continually risk testing this with others.

Peer group members trust that the presenter can discover and explore his or her own emotions, that the presenter is willing to delve deeper into the motivations for those feelings – the values, needs, and eventually standard – and that the presenter is willing to explore where God is working. They respect the presenter's process.

Monique started to relax. "Thank God, they are helping me look within rather than judge what I'm feeling as bad or good," she thought. She discovered that she needed the group to accept her and care about her needs, even when she was late, or didn't follow the rules.

In her supervision paper, Monique mentioned her stress and worry during the spiritual direction session. "When my directee talked about the issues she was having with her husband, my thoughts wandered to the fight I had with my husband the night before. I think I ruined the directee's experience. I felt embarrassed that she lost track of the conversation."

Sarah said, "What's that like for you, to feel embarrassed during spiritual direction?"

After consideration, Monique said, "Well, it's hard. I want to look good, to be treated with respect. But I see that my ego gets in my way and keeps me from looking at the truth. If I'm honest with myself, I realize that's self-centered. I'm not following God's standard when I stop listening."

Strength

In the Christ-centered model, strength comes from vulnerability, humility, and even humiliation. Peers and presenters alike advocate your position but combine it with inquiry and self-reflection. You recognize that feeling vulnerable while encouraging inquiry is a sign of strength.

More powerful group members realize that they are not always right, and that their voice should be heard after others, so they don't influence others. There is no winning or losing a conversation. Instead, focus is on following and acting like Christ.

Issues and feelings are not self-explanatory but instead evaluated in the light of truth and grace. Should the presenter feel uncomfortable, peers are missioned to explore that feeling. You can help by exploring the feeling to help clarify it, and by asking what value generates the discomfort. You want to discover where the problem lies. Explore the values that generated the feelings.

Logan, the most senior member of the group, said nothing up to this point. He wanted to be sure the others had a chance to comment first. "*That's a great observation, Ana, and it takes strength to say that, and understand what drives you. What do you see as God's standard in this case?*"

"*I want to let go of wanting to look good in the eyes of others and start depending on God completely for my self-worth. That would change my feelings. But I don't know how to do that.*"

Logan said, "We can switch to consultation right now if you like, so we can discuss some concrete ways to help you move in that direction. Would that be okay with you?"

Honesty

Seek free choice, informed by valid information. Encourage yourself and others to say what they know but fear to say. Recognize that "un-discussable" actions or feelings would otherwise be subject to distortion and cover-up.

It is important for all participating in supervision to voice honest feelings about the meeting. Platitudes and smoothing-over defeat the purpose of supervision. "Once his (the evil one's) tricks are revealed, his malicious purpose cannot succeed." (See [326] Spiritual Exercises of St. Ignatius Loyola.)[18]

"*I'd love some help, thanks,*" *Monique replied.* "*I was afraid to say what I felt, afraid I'd be judged. But now I see that when we bring a subject from the dark to light, like Ignatius says to do, it frees me. Thanks so much.*"

Integrity

Advocate your principles, values, and beliefs in a way that invites inquiry into them by members of your group. This stance encourages others to risk doing the same. Be committed to decisions and choices, and alert to ways they can be implemented.

Sarah said, "You are so welcome. I am grateful to you for your honesty, even when you are afraid."

Ana continued, "Last month, we reiterated that we would always follow Christ's standard and practice humility individually and in the group. I want to honor my commitment to those values. So, I'm asking you to help me learn some skills so I can stay more focused on my directee.

"Yes, we can move to consultation now to do that," Sarah replied.

Meeting Summary

At the end of every session, each group member is given the opportunity to express what he or she thought of the meeting, and how it affected them. Each person can identify a fruit of the Spirit that they noticed or improved upon. If a person was not enriched and blessed, the group should find out why.

It could be challenging for someone to be honest if they are concerned about chastisement for their response. So, promote the Christ-centered model even in the meeting evaluation.

Ana took a deep breath. She felt much lighter and freer once the session was done. The group provided some thought-provoking information and ways in which she could proceed. And she felt closer to them as team members and comrades. Next time she wouldn't be so afraid to talk about her deeper issues. She knew God was present. She felt enriched and strengthened. The Fruits of the Spirit that seemed most evident to her right then was joy and peace.

Facilitators

When you join or create a supervision peer group, it's important to have at least one person in the group who is experienced with supervision. This person should be present at every meeting, guiding, leading, and helping the group to stay focused on the presenter, to notice and mention when the group moves toward consultation, and to bring the conversation back to the presenter if it veers toward problem solving, or toward discussing the directee. These issues might seem obvious, and often they are. But many times, the group discussion veers slowly off track, toward those three main issues. An untrained supervisor can easily get caught in the momentum of the conversation and not recognize the direction until too late.

If you are a facilitator, pay close attention to the flow of the conversation. Should it tend toward discussion of any part of the directee's life or situation, steer it back to the presenter. Don't be afraid to interrupt (with love, of course) and return the focus to the presenter. You can say something as simple as, *"**Excuse me. We have drifted to the directee. Let's come back to the presenter.**"*

If you notice that any group member is giving advice, council, or methods for proceeding, stop the conversation to remind the group that you have moved into consultation. You might say, *"**I need to point out that we are now in consultation. Are we ready to proceed in that direction, or is there more to say in supervision?**"*

It is recommended and important that you focus on supervision before you enter consultation. You can read more about consultation in Chapter 19.

If the conversation becomes too technical such that it moves outside of the realm of spiritual direction and into chatting, problem solving, logistics, psychology, or other such topics, the facilitator must gently remind the group to return to supervision. A simple sentence such as "We are off-track. Let's get back to you, presenter," will return the group to supervision.

Facilitator Tasks

The most important task that a facilitator does is monitoring the conversation of the supervision session. As we've mentioned before, supervision must stay focused on Christ's standards and on the presenter. Should the conversation veer toward solving a problem of the directee, or exploring the life, habits, motives, or actions of the directee, you as facilitator must stop such a direction quickly. Gently interrupt (or even bluntly if needed) and redirect focus onto the presenter. Also, you as facilitator can acknowledge that the conversation is now consultation rather than supervision. You can decide if you want to continue in consultation and ask the presenter if that is okay or return to supervision. This is a learned skill. Every group member should be aware and open to mention any shift should it happen.

Other tasks that a facilitator might perform include:

1. Ensuring that the group maintain the Standard of Christ in every conversation.
2. Organizing the group – sending notices and keeping schedules.
3. Helping new members understand the dynamics of the group.
4. Stop any group member from stepping in as guru or savior. Learn how to stop such discussion firmly but graciously, and don't be afraid to redirect.

Summary

At the end of a meeting, allow each person to express how the meeting when for him or her. What did he or she learn? What felt challenging? What felt grace-filled? How could the group do better to help the presenter improve spiritual direction? What Fruit of the Spirit did they recognize?

When participants experience feelings of poverty of spirit, humility, and humiliation, they are working in a Christ-centered model. If people feel self-righteous, smug, irritated, belittled, angry, or placated, the group should readdress values, goals, and methods.

Questions for Review

These questions can help you identify how well your supervision session created a Christ-Centered environment.

List helpful and harmful aspects of your supervision process.

1. What helps the presenter to be open and honest, even with difficult or self-revelatory subjects?
2. What can you do to assist the presenter to stay focused on Christ and less focused on defending ego or self?
3. How will you promote the Standard of Christ in your next supervision meeting?

5 Affectivity

To be successful in supervision, either as presenter or supervisory team member, it is essential for you to know what causes your affectivity (the ability to experience positive or negative feelings and to react to them.) This understanding will assist you in spiritual direction. You will be able to take responsibility for your own affectivity and you will have the skill and understanding to help directees do the same. This is a life-long pursuit that will improve over time.

Perhaps because understanding affectivity is important in spiritual development and discernment, it is often downplayed, ridiculed, or ignored by almost everyone else.

It is vital that you understand affectivity and learn to appreciate your own responses to circumstance. Affectivity is what drives discernment and thus, spiritual direction. Affectivity comes from within – from the standard of Christ or the Standard of Evil (World, Flesh, Devil). Without understanding affectivity and addressing it, you can't discern, direct, or supervise well.

Understanding How Culture Trains Us in Affectivity

The cultural, nonspiritual world, trains us to find solutions, direct outcomes, and push those who stray from the norm to get back on track. spiritual directors don't push or solve problems. Instead, the spiritual director guides a person toward God, the ultimate solution to every problem.

Some people are tempted to "protect" others from further stress or trauma by avoiding any discussion of the difficult subject or emotion. Such tactics are not helpful in spiritual direction. Spiritual Directors are not protectors. You are called instead, to help guide directees toward God, the ultimate Protector.

Our culture, our families, and many internet sites indoctrinate us with the lie that your feelings come from outside of you – from others, circumstances, events, the weather, and any other aspect of life. Feelings are thus unpredictable and scary. Perhaps you were taught to blame circumstances or others for our feelings. If so, this book will introduce you to a new way to understand feelings.

In a small book, **The Way of Love,** Anthony DeMello, SJ writes, "Look at your life and see how you have filled its emptiness with people. As a result, they have a stranglehold on you. See how they control your behavior by their approval and disapproval. They hold the power to ease your loneliness with their company, to send your spirits soaring with their praise, to bring you down to the depths with their criticism and rejection. Look at yourself spending almost every waking minute of your day placating and pleasing people, whether living or dead."[19]

Some old popular songs say, "I *can't help* falling in love with you," and "You *make me* feel brand new." And if you haven't said these clichés yourself, I'll bet you've heard such comments as: "You make me so angry." Or "That makes me happy!" The common phrase, "That is so nice" places the value of nice on some action or item rather than attributing the "niceness" to the person who performed the action. We hear those and many more expressions daily that reinforce the notion that we are not in charge of our feelings. The cultural lie is huge and pervasive. Here's how the lie proceeds:

First, we are told over and over the falsity that feelings come from outside of us. This could be simply from the weather like rain or snow, calamities like hurricanes, actions of others, or even events we read about. I'm sure you've heard others say things like, "This day is so dreary it makes me depressed." Lyrics to **Rainy Days and Mondays** by the Carpenters say those two days always "get me down."[20]

If someone cuts in front of you on the highway, you might be in the habit of blaming the driver for your anger. You've surely suffered blame from others for their negative emotions. ("You should be ashamed of yourself!") Perhaps this produced shame or guilt in you, even if your words or actions were not meant to inflict any pain.

Second, you have probably been told from infancy that you can't change or generate feelings. They "just are" and so you must manage them by stuffing, ignoring, or venting. Most likely you have learned, when overwhelmed by unwanted emotion, to curb antisocial actions such as physical or emotional abuse or name-calling. You probably learned not to hit others when you feel angry, for instance. But our culture says it is okay to curse the weather or errant driver and love the person who 'makes' you feel good.

Thirdly, since our culture pushes the lie that we have no way to control feelings, we learn that the only way to prevent unwanted feelings is to impose control over how others act or respond to us. It's simple. Others must change so we won't feel what we don't want to feel.

I'm guessing that most people that live in the USA have internalized this mindset, but you as a spiritual director and peer supervisor must rise above the cultural standard and find what

God says about affectivity and incorporate that into your prayer, life, and spiritual direction.

Responding to Feelings

From childhood, you have been taught by parents, teachers, relatives, friends, and siblings (and the rest of society) to repress or ignore feelings that don't fit someone else's idea of how to act. I've heard many parents say, "Don't feel bad," to a disappointed child. We say, "You make me feel (fill in the blank…" And thus we hand off responsibility for our feelings to others again and again.

Learning what not to do with affectivity is an important part of a child's socialization. But I'll bet you didn't get a good idea about what to do with your affectivity, especially if it was negative. As a child, I was punished for acting smug or proud. I learned to lie about my emotions or keep them hidden, especially the negative ones.

Eventually, as I lived out this lie, I came to realize that I was at the mercy of others, my experiences, and of the world around me. I felt manipulated by those things and people that "caused" my emotion. I ran away from others by living an imaginary life, saying what others wanted to hear but having little idea about who I really was.

The longer a person lives with such discord, the more frustration and disappointment mount. Trapped in a cultural lie, a person begins to believe they have no control over affectivity – sees no way to stop unbidden emotions. In such a situation, one might be tempted to run from family, job, or locale to escape negative feelings. Or one might resort to emotional shut-down, shame, depression, or self-loathing.

All these consequences scare most people so they build emotional fences. These could include anger, depression, control, manipulation, teasing, bullying, or hiding the true self and avoiding intimacy. While emotional fences might keep unwanted emotions at bay, they also avoid intimacy and self-awareness and prevent a person from learning healthy ways to deal with emotion. Eventually, this leads to feeling helpless and emotional immaturity.

Hopefully you can notice that ascribing feelings to factors outside of yourself does three things: 1) fosters helplessness; 2) removes personal responsibility; and 3) removes all ways to understand and change feelings.

None of these are useful for supervision or spiritual direction. All hinder the exploration of God within.

This is why you as a spiritual director need to unlearn how feelings come to be within you and learn how to find what God is saying to you through those feelings.

Feelings Come from Within

The website, counseling-matters.org, has this to say about thoughts and feelings. "Psychiatrist Aaron Beck developed Cognitive behavioural therapy (CBT) in the 1960s. He observed the link between thoughts and feelings and recognized that, in changing one, the other changed. He coined the term *automatic thoughts* to describe the emotional-filled thoughts that come unbidden, often bringing strong negative feelings. Beck realized that, often, the thoughts went unrecognized; clients observed only their feelings. Beck found that identifying and challenging these negative automatic thoughts was key to helping clients overcome their difficulties and reducing their distress." [21]

This psychiatrist was on the right track. But there is much more to feelings than just thoughts.

In her book, **Radical Optimism,** author Beatrice Bruteau reminds us that circumstances do not necessarily determine emotional well-being. It's up to us. She writes, "We like to attribute our depressed feelings to circumstances – and indeed there are circumstances under which some people have to live that are enough to depress anyone – but we also know people can make themselves unhappy in quite neutral circumstances, and on the other hand can rise above an unfavorable quality of life to be happy."[22]

Ignatian spirituality and the Spiritual Exercises of St. Ignatius teaches that affectivity is our response to feelings based on a person's needs and values. These in turn help you to discover what standard (Christ or Evil) you are standing under in any response to stimuli. In other words, your feelings and affectivity are not just accidental flairs or random responses that occur unbidden. Instead, they are signs of God's presence (or absence) in every action, every decision that you make.

Every emotion a person feels arises from internal values that are affirmed or not and needs that are met or not. Through Spiritual Exercises, I learned that I cannot control others or circumstances. I can control my emotions because God has given control of emotion and affectivity to the person who is experiencing them. And God, through prayer, can teach us how to do that.

As a corollary, the Spiritual Exercises also helped me realize that my actions, other people and their actions, or circumstances cannot 'make' me do or feel anything. What a relief that understanding brings. For me, freedom came when I no longer felt at the mercy of circumstance. I did not have to accept the sadness, sorrow, anger, or other feelings that I used to feel when things didn't go my way. I could change my feelings by changing my values. You can too.

Personal Responsibility

In the Spiritual Exercises, we learn from St. Ignatius himself that feelings arise from deeper values, needs. He spent a year in recovery from his canon wound, reading and praying to understand this, and fortunately, shared it with those who provide his Spiritual Exercises to others.

To become an effective spiritual director, and thus supervisor, and to practice supervision well, you must develop your ability to feel first, and then understand (inside yourself) from where your feelings arise.

What value or need do you have that is either thwarted or met, that causes your emotion?

Whose standard are you under when you feel this emotion?

Your first job as a spiritual director is: know yourself.

Exploring and deepening your affectivity allows you to change your emotional response to a stimulus as you change the standard out of which you feel. Your awareness deepens and your personal responsibility for your own feelings increases.

The concept that values, not circumstances, generate feelings is not new. As mentioned earlier, St. Ignatius knew and wrote about this more than 500 years ago. 1500 years before that, Jesus knew and spoke about it in 30 AD. "For from the heart come evil intentions: murder, adultery, fornication, theft, perjury, slander. These are the things that make a person unclean. But eating with unwashed hands does not make anyone unclean."[23]

In his book, **Choosing Christ in the World**, Fr. Joseph Tetlow SJ, writes about dynamics:

"When I say four dynamics, I do not postulate four "natures" dividing up humankind, or four "classes" of people. I am not talking about metaphysics; I am talking about behavior and its origins and consequences. I am thinking of four quite distinctive ways of human living, ways that overlap so that few of us are unmistakably living one and not the others. I am trying to describe four moving sets of awareness, perceptions, emotions, desires, energies, commitments, affects, actions, and habits.... The four dynamics comprise four "spirits" and we discern by figuring out which of the four dynamics a given desire, action, or habit rises out of or functions within. Does a desire to become a spiritual director rise out of Christian generativity (Christ life) or out of a desire to have stature in the Church (sarx), or out of a desire to further the cause of feminism (natural humanism)? Did an act of kindness to someone who has done you harm serve the purpose of forgiving an enemy from the heart (Christ life) or the purpose of "being nice" (sarx), or the purpose of getting necessary business done (humanism), or the purpose of revenge by heaping coals upon his head (the dark)?"[24]

If you want to change how something affects you (your affect, that is, your emotional response), work backward from the feelings to values, to dynamics. You will begin to understand where your affectivity comes from and how your standards create your emotional response. Here's an example to clarify how to go about this process.

At the end of the last session, Damien's directee said, "You are such a wonderful listener. I really appreciate you." Damien does not feel comfortable with the compliment. He feels incompetent and unworthy of any praise. On examining the wheel of feelings, Damien identifies his strongest emotions as self-doubt and embarrassment, so he begins there.

On the Two Standards Chart, (following) Damien starts at the bottom, to find his feelings. Self-doubt is on the side of evil. On the feelings wheel, embarrassment is rooted in fear. 'What am I afraid of?' he wonders.

With prayer and consideration, Damien realizes he's afraid of pride and self-importance, and feels a lot of self-doubt. He thinks that if he refuses compliments that will keep him humble. But that mindset also makes him minimize the value of God's work in him. With deeper prayer, Damien realizes that his emotional embarrassment is really twisted pride. And that, he finds, is under the standard of Evil. Now it makes sense. He's acting under the wrong standard!

Damien asks God to help him change his view of compliments. He realizes that when he follows Christ, he can accept complements as ways to glorify God. They help him and his directee acknowledge the gifts God has given. He also can humbly realize that the one who compliments is noticing God within.

The next time someone complements Damien, he prays for humility. It is much easier to accept the complement. He can now honestly say, "Thank you for the compliment. I thank God for that gift and I'm glad it blesses you."

Now that Damien changed the standard under which he sees the compliment, he does not feel embarrassment. Instead he feels gratitude for God loving and affirming him through the other.

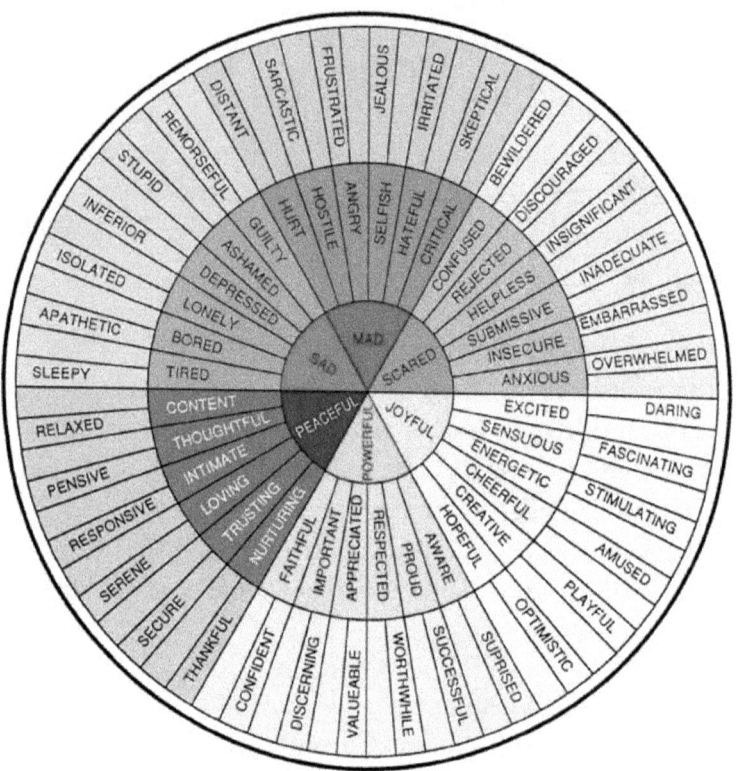

Figure 1 – Circle of Feelings

The chart on this page outlines how standards determine the dynamics under which we live. The dynamics form values and standards, which in turn generate feelings. To see how this works in supervision, let's use Monique again. In this example, Monique has been praying for insight to discover her own aff
to
gra
in

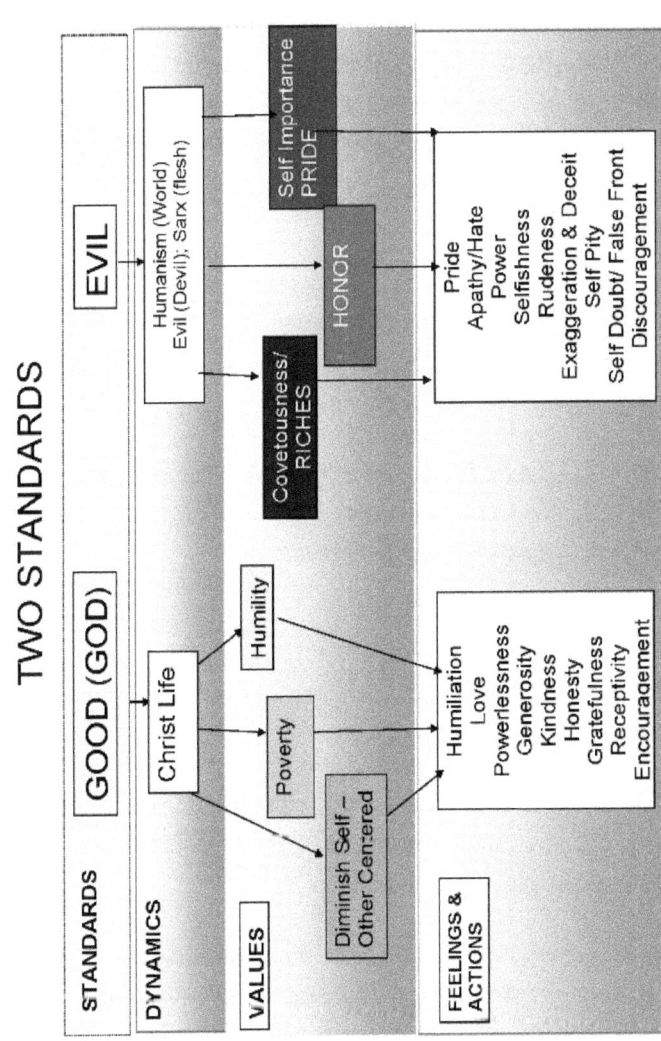

fol
Sa

Code Name: R; This was our 6th meeting.

Background

I have been meeting with this retreatant for about 8 weeks. She is faithful to spending time in prayer.

Statement of Intent
I am bringing this to supervision because I want to explore my ability (or lack of) to accompany my retreatant as we move from her thinking about Jesus to entering a heart-felt experience of Jesus.

Verbatim

R1: I love daily Mass the short sermons Fr. gives. He always asks a great question and I think about the question throughout the day. His questions are like what I'm praying about.

DIRECTOR AFFECT (DA): *This isn't what I expected to hear and am feeling disappointed. I hoped by now she would be experiencing Jesus more personally.*

D1: Can you tell me more about what happens in your prayer?

DA: I am not sure that this is the right question but want more insight into her prayer.

R2: Well, I often contemplate the trick questions that a Pharisee posed, or some nugget of insight from the sermon. But I am not watching the clock like I used to.

Now the conversation changes. The left side shows Monique's prior way of interacting. The right side shows how understanding affectivity leads the session in a new direction.

Old Way of Directing – focused on readings, etc.	New Way of Directing – focused on Affectivity
DA: I feel insecure. She seems focused on thoughts. I'm unsure how to guide her.	*DA: She is focused on thoughts. I'm unsure how to guide her but will try.*
D2: Have you ever had an experience when you encountered Jesus in a heartfelt way?	D2: Not watching the clock sounds interesting. Tell me more. Do you have any feelings about not watching time?
DA: I want to help her draw closer to Christ.	*DA: My question sounds odd to me. I feel hesitant but trust God.*
R3: Well, I don't think I've felt the presence of Jesus the way you describe. But I'm learning a lot. I usually just scan the stories. I know them all well.	R3: Well, I don't know… I usually just scan the stories. I know them all well so I don't need to spend a lot of time on them. Maybe peace? My prayer time is peaceful.
DA: thankful for her honesty but concerned. Where is Jesus?	*DA: I want to help her focus on peace instead of knowledge.*
D3: Have you tried applying your senses to any of the stories? You can follow the handout we gave you.	D3: Peace. I like that. How is that for you, to feel peaceful during your prayer time, even though you know the stories?
DA: My feelings of insecurity and inadequacy don't subside.	*DA: Yay! I noticed one feeling and called it to her attention.*

R4: *The conversation continues about readings, and sermons, and other thoughts that the directee has. R never talks about her affectivity.*	R4: It's no big deal…. (she thinks a moment) but I guess I enjoy the peace. It keeps me coming back. It's much better than being frustrated and ready to quit, like I was in the beginning, right?

From here down is a continuation of the right-sided conversation.

DA: *[I smile at her ability to tease herself. There's some humility here.] It dawns on me that we both easily miss seeing feelings, or we explain them away. I don't want to be distracted by her distractions or negative emotions. I'll stick to the positive.*

D4: Tell me more about that enjoyment. Can you identify what value you might hold that could generate joy in the peace in your prayer time?

DA: *She is talking about parts of her that I never noticed before. Hopeful.*

R5: Now that I think about it, my prayer is more than just sitting and thinking and not watching the time. It is quiet, and like an oasis. Jesus and i talk things over. I give God the credit for this. I'm trying to give him control of my life.

DA: *Values and dynamics are clarified. Great. This helps me to know what to ask next.*

D5: Giving Jesus credit and control are lovely gifts!

DA: *It gets easier to deepen discussion of feelings and affect once I realize they are coming from within her.*

R6: [Moving to the front of her chair, talking with her hands, smiling] I never thought of it this way before, but yes, when I give up control to Jesus, I'm happier.

DA: Wow. We've never talked about this in such depth. Thank you, Jesus and supervision group, for helping me.

D6: What a deep understanding and great blessing – peace and joy together.

DA: I'm awed by what God has done here.

Summary

Your feelings arise from your standards, where you are following either God's standard or the standard of Evil (which, as we said before, includes sarx, humanism, and evil, better known as the world, flesh, or devil). Once you know and live this, your life as a spiritual director will be easier. You will understand that you can help a person identify God's voice in their life by looking for feelings, that define values and needs, that point directly to the standard of either Christ or Evil.

Your job of the spiritual director is to help your directee explore the depths of his or her soul to locate God. Supervision will improve your ability to identify your own feelings, where they come from (within your own heart - values, needs, standards) and how to choose Christ and His standard so that you can change your feelings.

Standards Exercise

Unless you know and practice this yourself, you won't be able to help your directee understand let alone practice this method of understanding self and discernment.

Try this:

1. Spend time in prayer asking the Lord to enlighten you about what you are feeling.
2. Record a few of your current feelings. These don't have to be major. What are you feeling right now?
3. Once you have a few feelings listed, choose one to focus on.
    a. If the feeling is negative, ask yourself: "What value or standard do I hold that is not being met or is ignored in this feeling?
    b. If the feeling is positive, ask yourself: "What value or standard is being upheld or met as I feel this feeling?
    c. There are often two or more values and needs that work together to generate a feeling. Keep exploring until you've encountered at least two different values.
4. Once you have identified values and needs, determine which standard you are working under.

6 Discernment Guidelines

One of the most important aspects of spiritual direction involves discernment. You as spiritual director, are missioned with helping your directee find God's will. With the discernment guidelines, you will have tools to help you direct a person deeper, where they can discover what God is saying and urging at every moment.

To be a good spiritual director, then, you must know the rules of discernment well enough to instruct your directee about those that are needed at any given circumstance during spiritual direction. These rules have been identified by St. Ignatius Loyola in the 1500s, gleaned from the scriptures and from prayer. They are taught to people who pray through the Spiritual Exercises of

St. Ignatius, either the 30-day retreat or the 19th annotation, Retreat in Everyday Life.

David Fleming S.J. in his book, ***Draw Me into Your Friendship***, writes this about discernment guidelines of St. Ignatius. "The statements below are an attempt to present certain norms which might clarify different interior movements which happen in the human heart. By the grace of God, we are meant to recognize the influencing powers by evaluating those motions which are good so that we might let them give direction to our lives and those which are bad so that we might reject them or turn aside from them." [25]

There are two sets of rules for decision making. One applies when choosing between good and evil. The other applies when choosing between good and best (God's will). Each has different "rules" and considerations. This book will number the rules based on St. Ignatius' Spiritual Exercises, so in some cases the numbers will not be in order.

These rules are paraphrased and summarized from the book, Draw me Into Your Friendship, by David Fleming SJ, PhD.[26]

Part 1 – Guidelines for Choosing Between Good and Evil

Terms needed for Discernment

Consolation and Desolation are terms that describe the inner life. Every discernment starts with identifying the attitude and circumstance of the inner life. The rules that apply to these terms will be listed first.

Rule 1.3. Spiritual Consolation

Consolation can be found in any increase of faith, hope, or love -

a deep-down peace. Here are some ways to recognize consolation in my interior life:

- I'm on fire with the love of God, and nothing keeps me from giving my total self to God.
- I'm sad, even tearful, for being unfaithful to God, yet thankful for salvation.
- I realize I am a sinner before a loving God.
- I am grateful for Christ's love for the Father, for me, and others.
- Any other reason that leads me to praise, thank, and serve God more deeply
- When I feel strengthened in life, faith, hope, and love and bold with joy of serving God.
- God alone brings consolation without · cause (that is, input through our senses, experiences, or actions).

Rule 1.10 – When enjoying consolation, savor the strength you gain for the future should consolation leave you.

Rule 1.4. Spiritual Desolation

Desolation is an inner attitude when we find ourselves enmeshed in diminished connection to God. Here are some signs that a person is in desolation.

- You feel disconnected from God, as if you are left to fend for yourself.
- You feel spiritual turmoil or weighed down.
- You lack faith, hope, or love.
- Spiritual activity (including prayer) feels distasteful.
- You feel restless and uninspired in your service to God.
- You feel rebellious, despairing, and/or selfish.

- You feel little or no support or sweetness of God's love.
- You lack fervor in my response to God.
- You feel bland, and/or dull.
- You feel spiritually flat.

Rules 1.5- 1.9, 1.11. What to do in Desolation

Rule 1.5. In desolation you should hold fast to the decisions that guided you during the time before desolation appeared. This is very important, but often difficult and counter-cultural.

Rule 1.6. Although you don't make new decisions in desolation, you do not sit back and do nothing. You must pray more or intensify prayer, do penance, and make an examination of self, life, and faith. Practice patience and wait for consolation.

Rule 1.7. In desolation, you might feel as if God has abandoned you. But by faith, you know God is always with you. In the times of desolation, you might not experience sweetness of divine love and your response might lack fervor. Pray anyway.

Rule 1.8. In desolation, it is important to practice patience, which can mitigate frustration, dryness in prayer, or empty feelings. Try to recall past consolations and remember that consolation will return.

Rule 1.9. Desolation is not evil. It is not something to be abhorred or rejected or avoided at all costs. It is a gift. It teaches many things. There are three important reasons that a person suffers desolation.

a. Desolation is your own fault because you have not lived a life of faith or you've slacked off.
b. Desolation is a trial allowed by God. In desolation you are

tested as to whether you love God or just love the gifts of God. (Do you love the consolation of God, or God of consolation?)

c. Desolation gives you time to understand your own poverty and need for God. Desolation helps you see more clearly that consolation is gift that you can't buy, make, or control.

Rule 1.11 – In consolation, learn to grow in humility. Acknowledge gifts, be grateful for grace and recognize God's favor. In desolation, take some consolation in knowing God's grace is enough to follow the Lord. Trust that consolation will return.

Rules for Choose Between Good and Evil

Rule 1.1. If you sin, (**choose evil over good**) — perhaps you continue a bad habit, live out a character flaw, engage in sinful thoughts or actions— the evil spirit rewards you of sensual pleasures, so you'll increase your vices. In this circumstance, when you sin, God pricks your conscience through your reason to get you to change from evil ways. *(You think: "I know this is wrong. I feel guilty.")*

Rule 1.2. If you are trying to **choose good over evil— tactics of evil are opposite from rule 1.** The evil spirit will try to discourage or confuse you, rouse false sadness for things missed, instigate anxiety about persevering when we are weak, and suggest roadblocks to following Christ.

In contrast, when you decide to choose Good, God is very gentle—comforting and encouraging you. God holds you lovingly and makes things clear. You feel peaceful, cheerful, and simple. The Good Spirit gives strength, courage, consolation, inspiration, peace and firm resolve.

As you find yourself in a First Week decision (between good and evil) here is how you recognize the tactics of evil.

Rule 1.12. Evil acts like a spoiled child, irritating, bothering, and tempting us to sin. To avoid desolation during this tactic, don't be indulgent or weak. When you see the devil stomping his feet or luring you with false affection, be firm. Set limits. Say no.

Rule 1.13. Evil acts like a false lover; the devil uses you for his own selfish ends. Evil usually suggests that you keep the sin or intimacy a secret. To avoid desolation, do not keep secrets. Instead, talk to a confessor, spiritual director, or friend about temptations, decisions, suggestions, and desires. Even if the secret seems self-incriminating, tell someone you trust.

Rule 1.14. Evil acts like a shrewd military commander (2 ways):

a) Evil carefully maps out ways to attack fragile, weak, or unprepared defenses. This is less serious since you might more readily acknowledge your need for God's help.
b) Evil twists pride to work against you. You begin to think you don't need God's help – you've got this (feeling smug). This is the favored tactic of evil.

Part 2 - Guidelines for Discernment of Spirits - Between Good and God ("2nd Week" Decision)

The following statements are meant to help you understand interior movement which are part of the spiritual life. These guidelines are more subtle than Rules 1 and 2. These guidelines are important to understand and commit to memory so you can explain each one to any directee you might have.

Rule 2.1. When you are **trying to choose between good and God**, God and his angels tend to give support, encouragement, or even delight.

When you are **trying to choose between good and God**, the evil spirit generally tries to make you feel dissatisfied, anxious about God's love or your response, or he stings your conscience with thoughts of pride about your attempt to lead a good life (desolation).

When trying to choose between good and God, the movement of the good spirit is delicate, gentle, or delightful. Compare it to a drop of water on a sponge (no splash). When the evil spirit tries to interrupt that progress, the movement is violent, disturbing, and confusing. Compare it to how water splashes when it hits a stone.

Rule 2.2. God alone brings consolation without any cause. If you feel consolation "without cause" (which means you didn't have any special thoughts, achievements, events, prayers, or people to create the consolation) consider it to be from God. God alone brings consolation with no outside stimulus.

When consolation comes "without cause" be very careful to separate actual consolation from its afterglow. You might feel joy and exhilaration for a while. This could prompt you to do something for God. Be careful. Your human reason influences your consolation and decisions. After a consolation without cause, consolation is not just from God anymore. **Never decide in the "afterglow."** Discern good and evil very carefully before you make any a consolation without cause, consolation is not just from God anymore. Never make a decision in the "afterglow." Discern good and evil very carefully before you make any decision after consolation "without cause."

Rule 2.3. When you are **trying to choose God over Good**, and you have consolation "with cause" — consolation brought on by certain thoughts, achievements, events, or emotions — then consolation can come from the evil or the good spirit. The good spirit brings consolation that strengthens and speeds our progress to Christ.

The evil spirit, on the other hand, arouses good feelings (coming as the angel of light) so that we are tempted to focus on wrong things, pursue a selfish motivation, or place our own will before that of Christ. The movement from Christ-centered living to evil-centered living usually happens so quietly and slowly we sometimes don't notice until we have gone a long way in the wrong direction.

Rule 2.4. For a person striving to lead a good life, **trying to choose God over Good,** the evil spirit ordinarily appears as an angel of light (good). For example, you might be inspired by "holy" thoughts or desires. But over time, you find that actions based on those inspirations lead to pride, selfishness, or preoccupation so that your relationship with God diminishes. Or you don't accomplish what God really calls you to do. Looking back, you can see evil was disguised as light.

Rule 2.5. In decisions where you are **trying to choose God over Good,** examine the beginning, middle, and end of your experiences. This gives perspective; helps you see if you are following Christ in the end.

If, in reflecting on your thoughts, feelings, and actions from beginning to end of a decision, if you have remained focused on the Lord, you can be sure that the good spirit had been moving you and the decision is sound.

If, however, when you examine the beginning, middle, and end of a decision, you realize that you started off well but your thoughts and actions became self-focused or turned you away from God, suspect that the evil spirit has twisted a good beginning to an evil direction, and possibly even to an evil end. Any weakened spiritually, desolation, or confusion over time is a clear indication of the evil spirit's influence.

Rule 2.6. If you realize that the evil spirit duped you (you chose a "good" that led away from God), you should carefully review all stages through which you passed. Start from the time you noticed the evil (or desolation) and trace back to the good to find where you went wrong. Do this to decide what to do now to get back on track, and to help you be on guard in the future.

Rule 2.7. As you continue progressing toward God, the Good Spirit is delicate, gentle, delightful. The Good Spirit touches us like a drop of water penetrating a sponge. When the evil spirit interjects, it is more like water hitting a stone. For persons going from bad to worse, the descriptions are reversed.

Rule 2.8. When consolation comes directly from God, there is no deception in it. However, you need to be very careful to distinguish the actual moment of consolation from the afterglow of exhilaration and joy that comes from it. Help any directee distinguish between these two types of consolation, so that they do not make decisions influenced by this afterglow. Be very careful to help your directee discern good and evil spirits before any plan of action is formed.

Chart of Discernment Rules

As a spiritual director and supervisory team member, you are missioned with understanding and even memorizing the rules for discernment so that you can help any directee clarify the flow of the process and give you some new ways to consider any decision.

In every supervision paper you write, you will be asked to identify which rule of discernment you used or mentioned in spiritual direction. So, take the time to study them, know them now, and refer to them often.

The following flow chart can help organize many of the discernment rules on one page for easy reference.

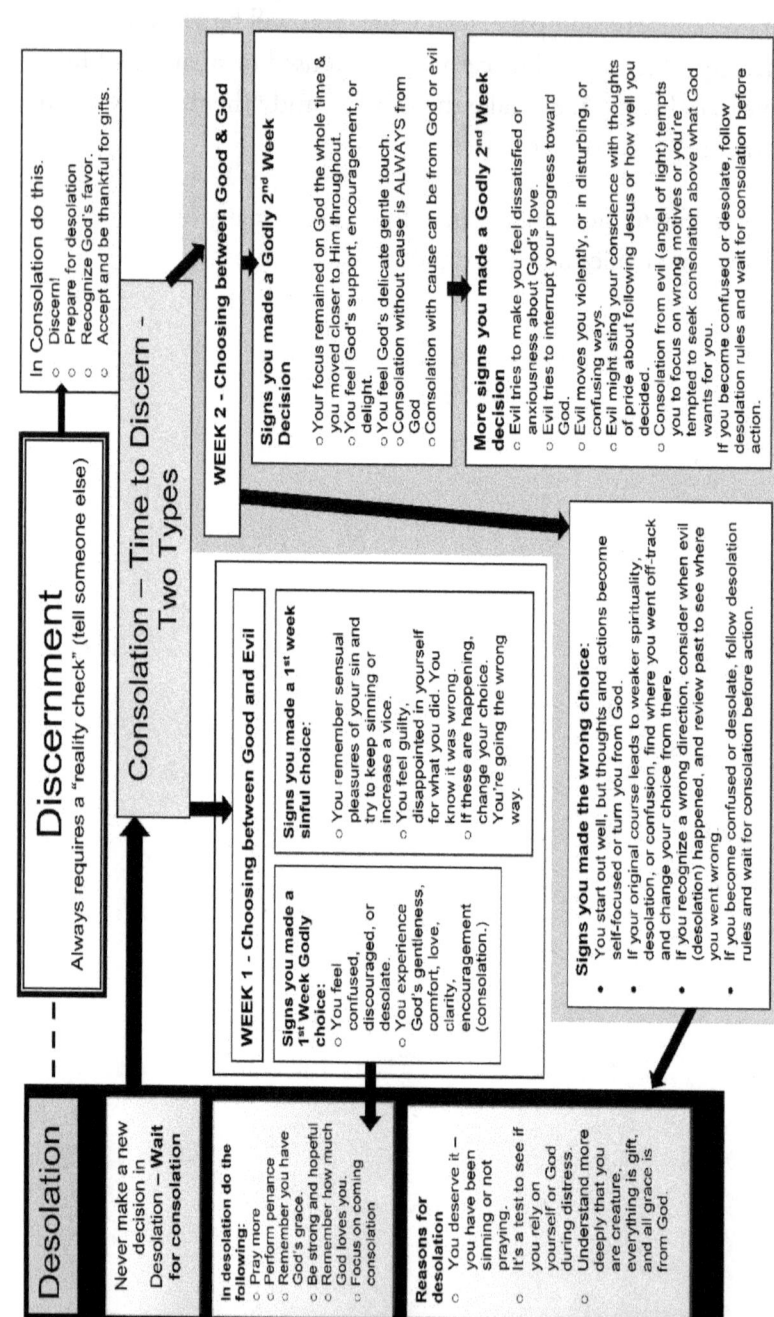

Section II

Tools for the Supervision Presenter

7 Christ-Centered Model as Presenter

In his book, **The Holy Longing,** Ronald Rolheiser says, "If it is true that we are the Body of Christ, and it is, then God's presence in the world today depends very much upon us. We must keep God present in the world in the same way Jesus did."[26]

Our job as spiritual directors, as supervisors, and as Christians, then, is to live as close to Christ's standard as possible. But to do so is not always intuitive or easy. Fortunately, you have the blessed opportunity to practice supervision that teaches you how to perform self-evaluation and growth. Supervision makes living out your mission as spiritual director easier and helps deepen your ability to be present.

To be well-supervised and to supervise well, you need to practice self-care and self-discipline.

First and foremost, deepen your personal prayer life. Secondly, meet regularly with your own spiritual director, and thirdly, be supervised regularly. These three aspects – personal prayer, spiritual direction, and supervision – work together to ensure that you as spiritual director stay focused on God.

Confidence - Spend some time in prayer to clarify the nature of your confidence (if any) or lack thereof. If lack of personal confidence causes you to experience undue hesitancy, turn to Christ. If you feel over-confident in your own abilities such that you don't depend on God, turn to Christ. If you exhibit courageous humility and personal surrender, you are in the correct frame of mind. Let God be in charge.

Humility - Come to supervision with a commitment to be as open as possible. Practicing humility and embracing humiliation make for good supervision. (In Ignatian spirituality, this is part of Christ's Standard). It is through humility and humiliation that we grow toward openness. Your job as presenter is to accept struggles or mistakes you've made humbly so the truth is uncovered. If you feel defensive, pray for help to embrace that with humiliation. You can also say to the group: "I feel self-protective, but I want to get to the truth. Help me put down my defenses."

Trust - Trust that others will love you through the process, no matter what. If you are new to a group, or just beginning as a spiritual director, this may take time. If you can't trust the group members immediately, be open about this, too. Say things like, "I'm nervous about sharing this." Or even, "I don't know if I can trust you all with this. It is sensitive." You might even say, "I am hesitant to do so, but I trust you all to hold this with gentleness and care. Please be gentle with me." Allow your group members to help you through difficult revelations and self-disclosures. Only with trust does one feel comfortable revealing faults and foibles.

Risk - Take a risk and say what you are most afraid to mention or talk about, where you feel embarrassed, or what you think will make you look bad or dumb. When we take what is in the dark and put it into the light, we prevent cover-ups, deception, and distortions. We follow one of St. Ignatius' rules of discernment: "our tactics must be to bring our temptations out into the light of day to someone like our director, confessor, or some other spiritual person."[27]

When we risk telling our story, revealing our vulnerabilities, or discussing a difficult subject, we bring Christ into the situation, and make ourselves more whole. That is why it's so essential to have a climate of acceptance in supervision. This makes sharing deeper and more real. Author Ronald Rolheiser puts it this way, "We have our sins forgiven by being in community with each other, at table with each other. Bluntly put, we will never go to hell if we are touching the community – touching it with sincerity and a modicum of contrition."[28]

Personal spiritual direction - Meet your own spiritual director regularly. This puts you in contact with another who provides by example different direction methods, along with an opportunity for deeper introspection. You will learn new techniques and gain a deeper understanding of the craft of spiritual direction. Plus sharing your faith journey will help you stay humble, open, and modest.

Meeting with a peer supervisory group further strengthens confidence and deepens insight into methods and motives.

All good supervision (and supervision presentations) starts with prayer. Prayer deepens our relationship to God. It is vital that every spiritual director prays daily. Pray before you meet your directee, that you will be a conduit to Christ. Then, once you begin writing a supervision paper, pray again. Ask for a deeper understanding of yourself, your motives, and your emotional response to your directee. Spend time contemplating stronger emotions, and your values and standards.

Attributes of Good Spiritual Directors

Good Spiritual Directors Pray

Prayer develops a relationship with God, which in turn keeps us engaged and praying. Prayer stimulates the desire to know God and allow God into our inner selves. The first part of the Spiritual Exercises of St. Ignatius, including the Principle and

Foundation, helps a directee deepen and broaden this enjoyment. You, as a spiritual director, are called to remember always that God loves you, including all your frailty and foibles. And as you consider this love God has for you, as you are, you can grow in love for God, for your fellow supervisors, and for your directee.

Your job as spiritual director is to love God, yourself, and your directees enough to desire personal change and growth. Learn to be thankful for everything, even your faults, so you can be transparent, open, and generous with your self-giving.

It's a strange and wonderful truth that as you deepen your self-understanding and acceptance, you diminish your self-centeredness. As you look inward to discover the places of pain, suffering, discord, untruth, and humiliation, you grow in love, honesty, and joy. And your self-inspection assists your efforts in helping a directee do the same. This is a great way in which you as spiritual director can "pay forward" the graces that you receive through prayer.

> *"The enjoyment of God should be the supreme end of spiritual technique; and it is in that enjoyment of God that we feel not only saved in the Evangelical sense, but safe: we are conscious of belonging to God, and hence are never alone; and to the degree that we have these two, hostile feelings disappear."* ~ Experience of the Enjoyment of God, as described by psychiatrist J.S. Mackenzie.[29]

Prayer is more than a way to deepen your understanding of self; it is more than just a useful tool for growth. Prayer is connection to God. If you learn to enjoy your time with God in prayer, you will deepen your joy. This in turn will deepen your desire for others to experience that same joy.

Supervision is one of the best tools that can help you open your spirit more fully to this process by helping you discover any impediments to God's invitation to deeper union.

Good Spiritual Directors Trust God

As we practice spiritual direction, we come to realize that we are wounded healers. We try to listen with open hearts and ears, and most of the time, do so. But because we are human, our inner lives can get in our way. Sometimes we are tired, distracted, unprepared, irritated, angry, or disillusioned. Fr. Tom Colgan, S.J., (Jesuits West) recommends that every spiritual director pray specifically before each spiritual direction session for the directee. "Each time you pray, you will get some guidance from God – a word or a concept for the person you direct. Sometimes I don't know what the word means until I'm in the session. So, I write that down." he says. "Later, God will remind me when I need it. This has been very important for me in my spiritual direction."

Good Spiritual Directors Evaluate Self

Who are you? Why do you want to be a spiritual director? What drives you to be open to others? These questions are important because as you deepen your understanding of yourself and your motives, you become more sensitive to the people you are directing. And to explore such questions, you must meet with our own spiritual director regularly.

In a blog post called **Self-Esteem and the Love of God**, Dr. Jeff Mirus writes about self-esteem. "Unfortunately, there are many reasons why a person might lack this sense of God's love, even if he or she has a deep religious faith. It can be caused in us by abusive parents or by divorce, by psychological incapacities of various kinds, and by our own sins—even if we are fighting with those sins. Like Adam and Eve, we sense our utter nakedness, and the Devil exploits our shame to make us hide from God (Genesis 3:10). Then there are people who are either ignorant of God or have been carefully taught to reject the very idea of God. Their sense of self-worth will necessarily depend on things which are far less sure than God's love."[30]

We as spiritual directors are in the business of helping our directees see God in all things: All things include every cell of every person, every action, every heartbeat, every breath. God is in ALL THINGS. If we ourselves can't see God in those moments, cells, and heartbeats, breath, how can we possibly help others see them?

Fr. Michael Esparza explains why God must be central to any conversation about self-esteem in his book, **Self-Esteem without Selfishness: Increasing Our Capacity for Love**.[31] Basically, we learn to accept our own faults and love ourselves when we recognize the infinite delight God takes in each one of us.

Good Spiritual Directors Embrace and Practice Humility

The virtue of humility may be defined as: "A quality by which a person considering his own defects has a lowly opinion of himself and willingly submits himself to God and to others for God's sake." St. Bernard defines it this way: A virtue by which a man knowing himself as he truly is, abases himself." These definitions coincide with that given by St. Thomas: "The virtue of humility", he says, "consists in keeping oneself within one's own bounds, not reaching out to things above one, but submitting to one's superior" [32]

The bible tells us in James 4:6 "God opposes the proud, but he gives grace to the humble."[33]

Isaiah 66:2 reminds us, "All of this was made by my hand and all of this is mine – it is Yahweh who speaks. But my eyes are drawn to the man of humbled and contrite spirit who trembles at my word."[34]

Proverbs 16:18 tells us, "Pride goes before destruction, a haughty spirit before a fall."[35]

To practice humility, we need to understand what it is. Dr. Orestes Brownson, on CatholicCulture.org writes, "The masters of spiritual life tell us that humility is not only a virtue, but the root of all the virtues, without which there is and can be no real virtue. Humility is not servility or meanness of spirit, but is real greatness of soul, and the basis of all generosity and disinterestedness. Pride, the vice opposed to humility, has no magnanimity, no generosity, is always cold, narrow, selfish, cruel. …The Christian rises above the world by his humility, not his pride…. He overcomes all the evils and mishaps of life, not by regarding them as trifles to be despised, but by regarding them as the loving chastisements of his heavenly Father, and by making them a means of spiritual progress."[36]

With true humility, we recognize all is gift, given by God for our salvation. Humility takes us to God. It helps us realize all we have is from God, and God should get the glory for it.

Humility is an important attribute that is necessary for every spiritual director to be successful in spiritual direction and supervision. A humble spiritual director is open to instruction or correction and can use the gifts God gives for the job of helping another person grow in love for the Almighty.

Good Spiritual Directors Embrace and Practice Humiliation

There are probably people in the world who like humiliation. For most of us, humiliation just feels embarrassing and objectionable. Some might even say they feel "disrespected" when they experience humiliation. Yet, if you are following the Christ-life dynamic, and trying to follow the standard of Christ, humiliation draws you closer to Christ. Spiritual directors focused on Jesus' Standard become better directors through humiliation. Supervisors, too, improve with humiliation. When we listen to God's call and embrace the humiliation, we can learn to appreciate humiliation's value, (even if we don't like it).

On the Vatican News Blog, Linda Bordoni quotes Pope Francis speaking about humiliation in a sermon.

"Sometimes we think that humility is to go quietly, perhaps head-down looking at the floor… but even pigs walk with their heads down: this is not humility. This is that fake, ready-to-wear humility, which neither saves nor guards the heart…. We must be aware that there is no true humility without humiliation, and if you are not able to tolerate, to carry humiliation on your shoulders, you are not truly humble: you pretend you are, but you are not." Pope Francis concluded by saying, "And if someone is brave – just as St. Ignatius teaches us – he can even ask the Lord to send humiliations so he can be more like the Lord".[37] Being a spiritual director requires this type of bravery.

Because you have been called to be a spiritual director, you are also called to explore the deeper aspects of your emotions and spirit. These might be joyful and uplifting, but chances are you'll discover many places that feel uncomfortable and humiliating. Supervision has a wonderful way of tunneling into our lives so that all aspects are open for view. During this process, a spirit of humiliation is the best way for you to ensure that you are focused on Christ, not on yourself.

Good Spiritual Directors Embrace and Practice Poverty of Spirit

Kevin O'Brien, JS, wrote in his book, *The Ignatian Adventure*, "All of us are called to 'poverty of spirit,' or **spiritual poverty**, which describes a stance of utter dependence before God, not in any demeaning, servile sense, but in the sense of the Principle and Foundation: God is God, and we are creatures created to praise, love, and serve God. Before all else, we depend on God for our happiness and fulfillment. While we are grateful for our talents, abilities, wealth, and achievements, we are free enough to offer them to the service of God and others and to let go of them when they get in the way of that self-giving. In short, poverty of spirit is an emptying of self so that God can fill us with life and love. Our prayer helps us grow in spiritual poverty and freedom. Christ is the model of spiritual poverty par excellence."[38]

This attitude of spiritual poverty is what every spiritual director must develop to be open to the Holy Spirit during spiritual direction. Developing poverty of spirit is vital for good spiritual direction and good supervision.

"What does a person lose in this poverty? What do I grow poorer in?" you might wonder. Fr. O'Brien says we "empty our hearts of self so God can fill us with life and love." This sounds great, but how does a person empty the heart?

You as spiritual director, can learn how to be poor in spirit by opening your heart to embrace humility, emptying of self, and giving. Fortunately, each of us is asked to do this in supervision. As you share your deepest emotions, responses, mistakes, foibles and follies along with your joys, accomplishments and energy, you grow poorer in spirit.

Sharing your deepest self in supervision will develop within you a generosity and openness so that your responses, actions, and thoughts become less self-protective, less directive, and more open to the truth and the Holy Spirit. As you deepen your poverty of spirit, you will grow in love for Christ, for yourself, and for your directees. The goal for supervision will be accomplished.

Good Spiritual Directors are Open

As you recall, the goal for supervision is always to assist you as spiritual director to understand yourself better. This is not so much for self-knowledge as it is to assist you in your walk towards Christ: when you are acting according to Christ's Standard, and where you veer towards the Standard of the World, Flesh, and Devil.

Practice openness. Decide before you enter supervision that you want to be open both emotionally and spiritually. Even parts of you that may seem embarrassing or uncomfortable to share are important to reveal. We are called to act as St. Ignatius bids us in the Third Kind of Humility [S.E. 167]. Bring your emotional responses, thoughts, reactions, and comments to supervision, regardless of how you think they make you look, so that your supervisory group can help you evaluate them.

Ignatius calls the Third Kind of Humility, the most perfect kind. He writes, "...to imitate and be more like Christ our Lord, I desire and choose poverty with Christ poor, rather than riches; insults with Christ loaded with them rather than honors; I desire to be accounted worthless and a fool for Christ, rather than to be esteemed as wise and prudent in this world. So Christ was treated for me [S.E. 167]."[39]

Your deeper self is not 'private' in supervision as it might be in your family or friendships. It is not yours alone. Because you are serving God and your directee in a very personal way, you must give all you have, including your 'privacy' to the service of your directee. Expect your reactions, comments, and responses to be part of any supervision presentation. Because it impacts the life and spiritual growth of another, you need to see your inner life as co-owned with your supervisory group.

This poverty of spirit will help you grow closer to Christ, richer in self-awareness, freer of attachments, and best of all, poorer in pride, honor, and esteem. You will begin to see how free you become by letting go of the "wealth" of self-protections that you've built up over time.

Again, your personal growth, understanding, and poverty of spirit is encouraged more for your directee than for your own self-knowledge. As you deepen your understanding of how attachments bind you, you will become better able to help others do the same as a spiritual director.

In summary, privacy in supervision means that what is said in supervision stays in supervision, so members don't talk about issues of anyone outside of the session. Privacy is also attributed to everything about the directee, whose information you are missioned to keep private.

Questions

1. Can I think of any more attributes that I should have to be a good or better spiritual director?
2. How do I see humiliation, and what do I feel about 'embracing' it?
3. How can I deepen my poverty of spirit? Do I want to?
4. Is my prayer life adequate to sustain my efforts as spiritual director?
5. What is my trust level with God? Do I trust God to protect me even when I feel humble or humiliated?

8   Transcribing the Direction Session

Keep a log of your spiritual direction sessions. After each spiritual direction session, transcribe a relevant portion of your conversation using one of the formats in the Appendix. If you record your conversation after each spiritual direction session, you will have several sessions to choose from when preparing for supervision. Such a written conversation is called a 'verbatim' (meaning word for word) conversation because it includes, to the best of your ability, the exact words that you and your directee used during a session.

Although you want to be thorough and exact in writing the verbatim conversation, you also want to be succinct and stay within bounds of confidentiality. Exact words may be easy to write when the speaker is succinct. But writing verbatim conversations gets more challenging when the speaker spouts long-winded monologues, disconnected thoughts rolled together, or discusses private actions or sins.

If any of these are true for your chosen conversation, you can condense a directee's conversation verbatim. Just be mindful to maintain the essence of the conversation. This will help the supervisors and you to clarify the intent and focus of the conversation.

Here are a few examples.

One of my directees said, "I feel depressed. When it gets gray out, that makes me feel sad. I don't know how to get rid of this feeling, the blues that come over me. My family is not very helpful with this. My grown kids have no patience for it. They just tell me to buck up, buy a light, or just get over it. My parents were hard on me when I was a child because I had this then, too. I shouldn't be here. I want to go south for the winter to help with this problem, but I can't get there this year. I have commitments at home – I shouldn't have signed up for that auction committee and we can't afford to go south this year. I haven't got the money because of the accident and house repairs. My Uncle George had this too. I think it's genetic. I tried to get over it on my own, and I'm hoping God will help me, but you know, prayer doesn't seem to be helping…"

When I wrote my verbatim for that discussion, I condensed it to this: "I feel so depressed. When it gets gray out, I feel sad. I don't know how to get rid of this feeling. [She talks for 10 minutes almost non-stop about family issues, living through the winter, childhood, family members who were depressed, etc.]" I'm hoping God will help me, but prayer doesn't seem to be helping."

As mentioned above in the chapter on confidentiality, you can also change the wording that a directee uses if his or her actual words could incriminate or break confidentiality.

For example, one directee said, "I have come to realize that I'm addicted to alcohol. I drink every night when my husband gets home. I thought I could let it go any time, that it wasn't a problem. But I never stop. The other night I tried but couldn't do it. My husband and parents drink, too, so to me it was normal. Until God started to nudge me about it. I didn't want to address this at first. I tried to avoid it, but when I was tempted to keep it from you, I decided I had to talk about it."

In supervision, I changed this section of the conversation to, "I realize that I have a problem – a big, disordered attachment. God started to nudge me about it. I didn't want to address this at first. I tried to avoid it, but when I was tempted to keep it from you, I decided I had to talk about it."

In this example, I took out the actual name of the addiction mentioned, to protect the privacy of the directee. I also excluded mention of spouse and parents normalizing the behavior, so that supervisors wouldn't be able to decipher the disordered attachment from the context. The intent of the paragraph is still the same and gets the message across without giving too much information about the directee.

Verbatim Conversation Format

You can use one of two formats for your verbatim conversation. These are found in this book's appendix. Whichever format you choose, be sure to <u>include your own feelings (your affect)</u> for each section of conversation. This is the most important part of this verbatim.

Recognizing and Recording Affect

We all act in ways based on patterns and habit. For example, when faced with embarrassment or threat to our way of understanding, to prevent humiliation or anxiety, we might become defensive. When we receive praise, we might feel affirmed and energized, and be more open to risk. Rarely does a person stop and evaluate such patterns and habits.

Defenses or other automatic reactions can keep us from uncovering the cause of our discomfort. We might even hide from ourselves the fact that we have such reactions. Perhaps we've been conditioned to believe that certain emotional reactions are automatic and universal so they can't be changed. Such judgements and assumptions hide the invitation to growth and holiness that God makes through every circumstance and struggle.

Fortunately, every time you record a spiritual direction session, or write a supervision paper, you are given the chance to evaluate yourself and your responses. You get the marvelous opportunity to consider how your formed habits affect others, how they might assist or hinder a person's walk toward God, and how you can grow in understanding through the process. This is a blessing and boon to your own spiritual growth as well as for your directee.

No matter what you feel during a spiritual direction session – bored, disappointed, excited, or enthused – you can bring that to supervision. Regardless of whether a spiritual direction session is difficult or easy, you can use what was said in any session for supervision. For instance, if a conversation seems to flow well, you can express your surprise, wonder, thanksgiving, or gratitude to God for such an experience. If you find the discussion challenging, you might feel energized, confronted, enthused, or drained. You can take any of those feelings to supervision, because your team can help you discover the need, value or standard you hold that prompted those feelings. Once you understand the Standard (God or not God) you acted under, you can decide to embrace or change it.

Defining Affect

The word 'affectivity' comes from the Latin word ***affectare***, meaning "to aim at," and ***afficere,*** which means "to work on." Merriam-Webster's dictionary defines affectivity as "the conscious subjective aspect of an emotion considered apart from bodily changes. It is also defined as a set of observable manifestations of a subjectively experienced emotion."[40]

Affectivity then can be a subjective experience and, at the same time, the feeling quality of a person. The words 'affectivity', 'affect', and 'affection' are used in Christian spirituality with varying meanings. As you explore affect and affectivity, this book will consider it as the conscious aspect and observable display of an experienced emotion.

Thus, as you notice and name emotions along with your value or desire for those feelings, you are identifying "the general name for the emotional or feeling quality of an experience, as found in pleasure, pain, including a variety of emotions, such as love, hate, fear, and anger."[41] In other words, you are describing your affect.

Fr. Joseph Tetlow, SJ, explains affect this way: "He (St. Ignatius Loyola) did not mean an emotion, merely, like the feeling of fear in the stormy dark or of hunger in the morning. Rather, any affect includes the valuing, feeling, and desiring that follows on a commitment."[42]

Recognizing Affect

The more you can be in touch with and write into a supervision paper your own affect and how a spiritual direction conversation affected you, the better your supervision session will be.

Don't include remembered affect like what your directee expresses. For example, in one supervision paper, a directee was quoted by his spiritual director as saying, "I lack gratitude to God, and that causes me to be prideful. I put myself before others."

The spiritual director wrote this as his personal affectivity: "I am guilty of that, too, sometimes."

In supervision, a group member asked, "Were you feeling guilty at the time?"

"No, I was feeling sorrow for my sin in the past, and hopeful because I don't feel guilty now," he said.

"You just described your affect – sorrow for past sin, hope for the present. Nice job."

The questions helped the spiritual director identify his true affect and realize he had not written his actual affectivity in his paper.

To clarify and describe current, relevant affectivity – how you are affected by your feelings that crop up during the spiritual direction session or afterwards – you can use these questions to assist you.

1. How did my feelings change my mood or response during this particular spiritual direction session?
2. Where did I notice a change in my way of proceeding 9f any) in response to my feelings?
3. What's my observation concerning my response to my feeling?

To identify your affectivity and where it comes from, spend some time in prayer. Ask the Lord to enlighten you. Pray about your affectivity relating to the conversation before you start writing any feelings. Considering your own affectivity while you try to help another person uncover theirs takes time and discernment. As you learn to separate your thoughts from your feelings, values, and needs, as well as separating your own interiority from that of the other person, you will uncover and discover your affectivity. Write about what you discovered.

Expanding Feeling Vocabulary

Although most people can recognize their basic feelings (sad, mad, glad, scared), many don't have a large feeling vocabulary. You as spiritual director must ensure that your vocabulary for feelings, emotions, and affect is larger than your directee. You can improve your vocabulary by spending time each day reviewing this circle of feelings. As your vocabulary grows, your spiritual direction sessions will improve because you will notice feelings as they arise and be able to help your directee expand their feeling vocabulary.

The reason you want to understand your feelings better goes beyond deepening self-knowledge and increasing your feelings recognition and vocabulary. Feelings and affect are major signposts that help you discover which of the Two Standards you are acting under at any given moment: God or Evil (World, Flesh, Devil).

Here are a few exercises to help to expand your understanding.

1. **Compare and Contrast.** Review the wheel of feelings above. Choose two feelings that are found near each other on the wheel (for example: intimate and loving, or selfish and jealous.) Define for yourself the differences and similarities of each word in the set you've chosen. If you don't know the meaning of the word or can't describe it easily, look it up so it's clear.

2. **Increase feelings vocabulary.** Review the Wheel of Feelings or the list in the Appendix. Try to recall when you felt some feeling that is listed there, but that you don't normally notice. Can you recall a recent time that you have you felt energetic, insignificant, playful, pensive?

3. **Use a feeling word daily** in conversation and in your prayer. Choose a different emotion each day. Write that feeling in your journal and explain when you felt it. Try to identify what value you hold that prompted that feeling. Keep a list of the feelings you discover. The more you understand and use feeling words, the better you will understand your affectivity. This will transfer to your spiritual direction practice and thus help your directees learn this skill also.
4. Consider one feeling that you identified during this exercise. What values generated it? Then honestly consider whether whose Standard they fall under – Christ or Evil. (Most of the time our feelings are generated from values of both Standards, so try to discover both.) If you uncover values under the Evil standard (SELF: world, flesh, or devil) pray to God asking how you can change your value so your actions and values fall more fully under the Standard of Christ.

The main point of writing what you discussed and how you felt during spiritual direction is for you to discover more deeply who you are and how you respond and react during spiritual direction so that you can better understand what Standard you act under at any given time.

These summaries help you prepare for supervision. You can use any one of them to write for supervision.

Practice Exercise

Write a summary paragraph for each of the following circumstances, as if you were recording it for supervision:

- Your directee starts talking about feeling distracted in prayer. One sentence later she shifts to her evaluation of a family event, returns to scripture for a minute, then gets sidetracked again, focused on a family member's actions at the event. She pulls out her journal and reads a sentence about the scripture. It reminds her of a conversation she had with her neighbor, which she describes.

- Your directee is angry with her mother who is being directed by one of your peers. Discuss her anger without mentioning who she is angry with.

9 Choosing a Session for Supervision

Now that you have written a summary, your affectivity and verbatim for every spiritual direction session you participate in, it will be much easier for you to write a supervision paper using one of them.

> In her book, **Looking into the Well,** Maureen Conroy mentions five areas of focus that can help a spiritual director choose which session to bring to supervision. These five areas include:[43]
> 1. the experience of interior movements;
> 2. the director's personal issues that are stirred during direction sessions;
> 3. moral, theological, spiritual, and cultural differences;
> 4. the development of a contemplative attitude and approach; and
> 5. the relationship between the director and directee.

Let's look at each of these to see how they might impact spiritual direction and thus be useful to bring to supervision.

Experience Interior Movements

You might experience interior movements either towards God or away from God during a spiritual direction session. It's good to be able to recognize that such movement happened, but also understand with direction your spirit went and why.

Some questions you might ask yourself include:

- Were there any significant moments where you felt God's presence more keenly?

- At any time did you notice when your emotions didn't match the situation - either too much or too little?
- Where did you experience the greatest emotion, whether positive or negative?
- Are there any situations where you felt confused, out of place, or uncomfortable?
- Were there places where you felt energized or enthused?
- Were there any moments you would like to celebrate?

Answers to any of these questions can be used to help you write your statement of intent. For instance, if your directee expressed a consolation, or a deeper understanding of prayer, you may feel energized.

Possible Personal Issues that May Arise

- Have you encountered any issues that seem to block or impede your open response to God?
- Did you personally experience a deep experience of God in a session that you'd like to celebrate?
- Were there any places in the conversation where you avoided exploring deeper or risky subjects?

Moral, theological, spiritual, and cultural differences

The contrast between your spiritual, theological, cultural, or moral perspective and that of your directee can be quite different and could cause stress within the relationship.

- Have you experienced a discord between your values and those of your directee?
- Are there theological differences between you and your directee that you struggle with?
- Money, background, upbringing, education, family of origin, and many other cultural differences can impact

the spiritual direction relationship. Have you felt such discord or confusion in your spiritual direction session, and if so where?

Deepening your contemplative attitude or approach
- Do you feel as if you are working too hard? Why?
- Which part of a discussion was life-giving, or failed to be?
- Have you encountered any unresolved issues that interfere with your ability to listen clearly without distortion? For example, I wanted my directee to look at this part of her experience, but I'm not sure why.

The relationship between director and directee
- Where do you resist a particular part of the directee's experience?
- Where are you resistant? Do you avoid letting your directee talk about any subject?
- Have you over-explained or talked to much in a particular session?
- Have you resorted to solving problems or giving advice?
- Do you lose focus or stop paying attention? If so why?

Once you've noticed, evaluate. Which experience do you think about a lot? Which is perplexing or stressful? Which is at the top of your consciousness? Are there any that you are excited to tell about? Or issues that repeat themselves over and over? Or is there one that jumps out at you because it's so unique?

After you've considered these questions and prayed about which session God wants you to bring to supervision, choose the session that seems most noteworthy and write about that.

Steps in summary

- Prayerfully reflect on God, directee, and self.
- Ask for a discerning heart.
- Use discernment rules to identify which spiritual direction session to choose.
- Write your statement of intent starting with: I am presenting a portion of this conversation because I ...
- Answer the questions on the supervision form.
- Write your verbatim conversation that illustrates why you want supervision in this area.

10 Writing the Supervision Paper

You've transcribed summaries of spiritual direction sessions and you've chosen one to use for your next supervision session. Whether a spiritual direction session is difficult, easy, or effortless, you can use what was said in any session for supervision. If a conversation seems effortless, you can express your surprise, wonder, thanksgiving, or gratitude to God for such an experience. If you find the discussion challenging, you might feel energized, challenged, enthused, or drained. You can take any of those feelings to supervision, because your team will want to know what need or value or even standard prompted those feelings. No matter what you feel during a spiritual direction session – bored, disappointed, excited, or enthused – you can bring that to supervision.

You as spiritual director are now called to rise above the training of our society, parents, school, and employers to allow God to direct you. Your supervisory group members have the beautiful task of helping the supervised spiritual director discover where his or her feeling comes from inside of self (not outside, not from circumstances or another person).

Preparing Your Supervision Paper

We all act in ways based on patterns and habit. For example, when faced with embarrassment or threat to our way of understanding, to prevent humiliation or anxiety, we might become defensive. When we receive praise, we might feel affirmed and energized, and be more open to risk. Rarely does a person stop and evaluate such patterns and habits.

Defenses or other automatic reactions to stimulation can keep us from uncovering the cause of our discomfort. We might even hide from ourselves the fact that we have such reactions. Perhaps we've been conditioned to believe that such reactions are automatic and universal so they can't be changed. Such judgements and assumptions hide the invitation to growth and holiness that God makes through every circumstance and struggle.

Follow instructions in the prior chapter to choose a recent direction session that seemed powerful, meaningful, challenging, or confusing for you.

After you have answered all the questions in writing, choose one of the two formats – paragraph or chart – (See Appendix).

Write a one or two-page verbatim (word-for-word conversation - at least five paragraphs for director, five for directee). Record a relevant section of conversation between you and your directee that highlights the issue(s) you identified in your focus question and your affect. Record for EVERY paragraph.

The supervision paper has three parts:
1. Answers questions about you, grace, prayer, and discernment rules.
2. Verbatim [words that were spoken by you and the directee during spiritual direction],
3. Your statement of intent.

I'll discuss how to begin and each part of the presentation separately.

1. Answers to Questions

As you begin your supervision presentation, be sure you follow the guidelines described in the chapter on confidentiality. Always use a fictitious name; change any identifying data (initials, name, occupation, location) for your directee. You must always preserve his or her anonymity. Include only enough information about your directee to provide an adequate understanding of the session. You can find the form in the Appendix: =

Using your chosen recent spiritual direction session, answer the questions for supervision, found in the format in the appendix. Please answer every question fully.

Discernment Rules

As you evaluate the spiritual direction session you've chosen to present. With one person it might mean something as simple as deciding between prayer in the morning or in the evening. One directee I had wanted to give her whole life to Christ, so when she ate lunch, or even if she did was part of her discernment. Another person might be in desolation that you help identify. Another could be feeling the lure of a bad habit, or the consolation of God in a positive choice. What was your directee was discerning? Identify the discernment rule(s) you discussed or used. Include the number (see Chapter 6) and explain how it fit into your spiritual direction.

More about Affectivity

Share **your own** spiritual concerns, experiences, feelings, faith, blocks, blind spots, gifts, discernment, confidence, and/or confusions in relation to the session with directee.

As you write your supervision paper, it is tempting, at first, to write what you've experienced in your directee. She felt sad about the loss, he was excited about his new job, etc. But your job is to rise above cultural understandings of affectivity, feelings, and what influences you during a session. You are sked in supervision to share **your own** affectivity. This means you share how your relationship with the directee affected you, your feelings, and your response during the spiritual direction session.

Supervision is not about your directee. YOU, the presenter, are the focus for supervision. But it's not easy to focus on self in this way. Our culture teaches us to evaluate feelings by looking outward, toward others and events outside of ourselves. To supervise or participate in spiritual direction, you must look within. I encourage you to avoid feelings based on the directee. Notice the difference.

Here's how it works. The directee says something that triggers a feeling in the director. The director reacts and a feeling arises (troubled, irritated, or enthused, etc.). Instead of attributing the feeling to the directee, circumstance, or the conversation, the spiritual director attributes feelings to personal, internal needs and values. Here's an example:

Martha (Directee): My mother-in-law backed into my neighbor's car yesterday, and guess what? She wanted me to go over and apologize for her. "No way," I told her. I am so thankful for prayer, because I prayed right then. It helped a lot. I was able to stop myself from telling her to grow up and do her own dirty work (which is what I would have said before.)

Tana's (spiritual director) affect: I feel compassionate. I've had similar run-ins with my own mother-in-law. But I also noticed my irritation and anger, too. Why? I, too, had to pray about my feelings. I discovered I'm angry about the times I let others dominear me or tell me what to do. I'm angry at myself for the times I don't set boundaries. And sometimes I feel helpless because I don't always know how to be assertive without feeling aggressive. I am surprised that this session brought up all this in me.

Director identifies those personal values and needs and helps the directee clarify if they are God-centered or self-centered.

Tana Affect: Going deeper, compassion is from God, I believe. When I think about my reaction it more deeply, I recognize some selfishness in me. I expect others to treat me with respect so I don't have to set boundaries or make waves by telling them what I need.

Tana was self-aware enough to recognize her values and standards. But not everyone can do that. If director can't identify the source of affectivity, or wants more clarity, the peer group members can help the director to uncover the deeper values and needs that drove the response.

Director-Based Feelings

Base your affect, your feelings on your own needs, values, and standards. Refrain from reporting feelings based on the directee such as, "I'm feeling sorry that she has to suffer like this." Or, "I'm curious why my directee would act that way." Or "I'm disappointed that she chose to cancel the appointment." Such feelings focus on the directee, not on your affect. Instead, listen and try to identify your needs, values and standards. You might write something like:

- *"I care about my directee, so hearing about her pain makes me sad."*
- *"I am thankful that I have experienced this too, so I could understand in a deeper way what she is going through."*
- *"I sympathize and feel amazed that Jesus is healing me through this encounter."*

2. Verbatim

Learn how to show, not tell the story of one specific spiritual direction session using the exact (mostly) words spoken by both parties. The conversation includes no interpretation or paraphrase, making it easier for the supervisory team to draw their own conclusions and evaluate the conversation in their own way.

Conversations can ramble, of course, even in spiritual direction. A directee may begin talking about prayer, slide into a family matter, discuss how health impacted that, and take a tangent toward her lunch with a friend. You as listener are charged with the task of keeping the focus on God and calling the directee back to the point whenever you can. You don't have to write all those details as you write your verbatim. You are free to summarize a rambling conversation into a focused paragraph or exclude the parts that diverge from prayer and God. If you are wondering, however, how well you did with a redirect, or you want some insight or assistance in doing so, you can include rambling conversations and your verbatim.

You'll find two variations of the verbatim form in the apendix: *Sample Verbatim Paragraph Style* and *Sample Verbatim Conversation Chart Style*.

Please write your verbatim following the outline given. This means you write at least ten sentences of dialog (verbatim conversation) including your affect for every paragraph. Follow one of the two examples for verbatim. Remember to include your affect. (For help, see the list in the Appendix or the chart in Chapter 5 - Affectivity, above.)

Don't use the directee's actions or feelings as the basis for your feelings. Learn how to avoid making your directee's feelings as your own.

As you prepare to write your verbatim, consider your attitudes, feelings and values honestly. Why are you curious about motives? Are you interested because you want control over the situation, and understanding gets you that control? Or perhaps you believe you can better help the directee move towards God if you understand what drives that motion. There can be many reasons you are interested in motivation. Take time to discover the reasons that come from within your own heart.

Once you have completed your paper, send to each peer group member for review before your scheduled supervision meeting.

3. Statement of Intent

Your statement of intent will prevent you from having the following conversation with your peers:

"What do you hope to gain from this supervision session?" I asked.

"I'm not sure. I brought this paper because it was my turn to be supervised," the director answered.

It's not easy to uncover why you are bringing that specific conversation or incident to the process. Yet this is one of the most important questions to answer. There is something important about that event that touched us or confused us or brought us to our knees before God. And one important aspect for supervision of any type is for the presenter to discern what he or she wants from the session. As you know, the focus for supervision should be on the presenter and the presenter's affect.

Your verbatim will be much more helpful to you, and much easier for your team if you formulate an explicit and relevant statement of intent. The more specific you can make it to the conversation you are presenting, the better your group can assist you.

Your statement of intent is the glue that holds the supervision session together. This statement tells your supervisory group members what you want to learn or understand. It helps supervision group members stay focused on your needs, so you get your questions or concerns answered. If you notice a problem or block in your relationship with a directee, identify and confront it with as much candor and openness as possible.

Presentations don't always need to contain "problems" to solve. If the relationship is going well, for instance, your paper may be affirmation and/or gratitude for this fact. You might even say something like: "I want to celebrate the breakthrough that my directee had and explore why I'm so happy about it."

Here are steps you can go through to formulate your statement of intent.

1. Pray

As you begin to formulate your statement of intent, pray for guidance. Ask God to reveal which part of your direction conversation you should bring to supervision. Prayerfully consider what fruits of the Spirit you've seen in the spiritual direction sessions you have recently participated in.

Where have you chosen to follow the Standard of Christ?

[As mentioned above, Christ's Standard includes loving, helpless, generous, kind, honest, grateful, receptive, real, selfless, encouraging, and humble.]

Where have you noticed (in yourself) evidence of the Standard of Evil? [Again, as mentioned above, the Evil Standard includes apathy, hunger for power, selfishness, rudeness, deceitfulness, exaggeration, self-pity, self-doubt, fake, selfish, discouraged, over-directive, over-caring, worried about doing it "right," and self-centeredness. Look back at the chapters on the two standards for more detail.]

Record what you've discovered.

Choose a conversation segment that exhibits one of the above fruits or one of the Two Standards.

2. Brainstorm your Statement of Intent

A statement of intent defines what you need from your supervisory group. You will need to write a statement of intent for each supervision paper. To write your statement of intent, complete the sentence:

"I am presenting this portion of the conversation for supervision

because...."

Your intent provides your supervisory group members with a direction and intent for supervision. It gives them a goal and focus for discussion so be specific.

To identify the statement of intent, first evaluate. You know some of the fruits you've displayed, and what standard you've followed. So, what do you want to uncover, explore, or accomplish? What do you want your supervisory group to help you with? What do you struggle with before, during, or after a spiritual direction session?

Sometimes it takes a long time to figure out what your struggles are, or what the main point of a spiritual direction was.

Examples - Statements of Intent

"I want to understand why I had such sudden movements of emotions. I felt really upset when I thought 'Juan' wasn't engaged, as if I was just helping him meet some obligation. Why did I get so offended by that?"

"I want to explore if I'm separate enough from the person I am directing and her issues."

"I need help to understand when my sharing of personal experience is useful to encourage or guide my directee and where it impacts boundaries."

"I want to celebrate how prayer has brought this directee and me both to humility."

"I want to rejoice in how God has touched my life through spiritual direction with this person."

"I want to understand my discomfort about engaging with this directee as I try to hold the line between my day job as mental health counselor and my role with her as spiritual director."

"This directee often seems somewhat delusional and psychotic. Help me clarify if I am feeling the presence of those evil spirits she talks about."

How to identify what you need from supervision

Identify your feelings

2 In prayer, evaluate the spiritual direction session you have chosen based on the Two Standards. Look at the content, themes, directee's religious experience, your frame of mind, and what you judged, thought, and felt.

3 Try to uncover your personal response or impression of how your directee acted or spoke during this session.
   a) Consider any issues that this directee brought up, or avoided, ignored, or deflected, and the emotion the directee expressed.
   b) Recall your response to any comfort, avoidance, or deflection that you encountered in your directee.
   c) Study the feeling wheel chart for more options. Jot down how you feel about <u>your responses</u> during the session.

Identify and name what you are feeling.

In which part of the conversation did you feel some emotion that was noteworthy? This means you identify <u>your own reactions</u> to the conversation you had with your directee.

Review your spiritual direction session to discover where you felt any of the feelings listed in the circle. Identify specifically which emotions you encountered within yourself and where in the conversation they came up for you. From those you've identified, choose one or two that stand out for you. If you don't understand why you felt as you did, or you were surprised by your affect, write your statement of need based on the feeling. Ask yourself the following questions.

- Is there anything I want to understand more deeply within myself - why I felt as you did and want to explore deeper or celebrate some breakthrough (in you)?
- What do I want the group members to help me uncover or celebrate?
- Do I feel compelled to move to new ideas, thoughts, or questions instead of slowing to celebrate God's great gifts as my directee experiences them? If so, why?
- When did I let my emotion and personal affect change the discussion? In what way?
- Where do I have difficulty identifying the values that generate my emotions?
- Are there places or subjects where I feel compelled to instruct or explain? What values do I hold that prompt me to do so?
- Does it bother me when my directee talks a lot and I can't say much? If so, why?
- What (inside of me) causes me to react negatively in a particular situation, topic, or conversation?
- Why am I so frustrated when … (fill in the blank.)
- Why do I want to fix or own my directee's feelings?
- Why is it so difficult to let go of my need to control and let God be in charge?
- Why do I want to protect my directee from harm, from consequences, or from negative emotions?
- What makes me think I can or should rescue my directee?
- How can I stop placating?

- Why am I hesitant to challenge my directee to go deeper?
- Why am I hesitant to remind or insist that my directee to pray for the agreed-upon time?
- Why did my spirit drift further from, or closer to God during the spiritual direction session?
- Where did I express my personal value judgement concerning a decision or action of the directee, and why did I do it.

Questions that could lead to Consultation

Sometimes a spiritual director does not know how to address a particular issue. If you find yourself in this situation, you can formulate your statement of intent based on a question for consultation. The peer team will supervise first before consultation, of course. Here are some questions that you can use to help you formulate your statement of intent. A question that prompts consultation begins with the words "how" or "what."

- How could I have helped my directee go deeper into an experience? Was I afraid of her depth of feeling and what I might find there?
- What should I have done to keep my own feelings out of the process?
- How can I improve my listening so that I'm able to better summarize what my directee says?
- How can I stay focused when I listen to this directee?
- What can I do next time that would help the session stay focused on what God is doing in the directee's life instead of goals or other issues?
- How can I break through the surface of what seems to be

going on, to get to the core of what God is really doing in my directee's life?
- I feel stuck about (name problem.) How do I deal with this issue so it doesn't trip me up next time I encounter it?
- What can I do to remind myself that I don't have to fix a problem that I recognize or that the retreatant expresses to me?
- What in me causes me to feel compelled to "fix" or meddle with what I perceive is 'broken' or off track?
- How can I keep myself from slipping into counseling or life-coaching instead of sticking with spiritual direction?
- I am too concerned with how to repair a person or action. Help me to discover my trust level with God when it comes to actions that seem wrong to me.
- I don't seem to recognize the emotions that my retreatant has, since he/she doesn't usually name them aloud. How can I more readily notice them?

You can also use the form in the Appendix to help you identify the intent for your supervision session.

4. How do you feel about your response? Why? Answer the question: what caused the response I had? You can bring your answer to supervision.
Based on the dynamics of the session and/or the dynamics of the directee's relationship with God, what do you need to discover about yourself and how you responded during this session?

To help you understand this process better, here's an example. *In spiritual direction, when Joanne asked what her directee, Zoe, was feeling about a particular scripture, Zoe said, "I really don't have feelings. And the ones that I do have don't last long. Mostly I just ignore them."*

When she first started directing Zoe, Joanne felt interest and desire to help. After several sessions, Joanne felt confused about how to proceed. She judged that she worked too hard and felt frustrated and helpless. This led to the temptation to persuade or teach.

"What's going on?" Joanne asked herself. "Why am I so easily influenced? Why am I tempted away from following my training?" Joanne tried to put her impression into words. She wrote: "I judge that my directee was hesitant to share her affect and closed to the process. I am disappointed that I can't get her to express more, and I am frustrated that my "tried and true" method of getting a person to address feelings isn't working. More importantly, I have some kind of ego thing involved. I want to be successful and useful in spiritual direction, and don't like it when things don't go the way I expect or when my directee doesn't appear to be progressing, in my estimation."

Joanne spent time in prayer. She had no idea what she felt about her frustration, other than frustrated! It seemed strange to evaluate that. But when she did, it helped her identify where her directee needed her help and where she didn't. Joanne hoped the supervision could help her to stop caring about her personal "success" as a spiritual director, or her need to be helpful, and listen to God.

Joanne discovered that when she stopped expecting the directee to fill her need, she relied on God more. She wrote this as her statement of intent: Why do I have such trouble letting go of my expectations? How can I be more flexible, and more open to the Holy Spirit?

Summary

Your statement of intent is an important aspect of your supervision paper. It gives the group a direction in which to proceed. It gives the process a focus and when the group focuses on what you need, you get more out of the process. Don't skimp on the preparation for this statement. Take your time and create a statement that will serve you and your peers.

Every time you write a supervision paper, you can evaluate yourself and your responses. This marvelous opportunity lets you consider how your habits affect others, how they might assist or hinder a directee's walk toward God, and how you can grow in understanding through the process. This is an amazing blessing, and boon to your own spiritual growth as well as for your directee.

11 The Supervision Session for the Presenter

You've done it! You've written summaries for each spiritual direction session, chosen one to use in a supervision paper, and now you are ready for the supervision session. If you are new to the process, are preparing for one of your first supervision sessions, or participating in supervision using this method focused on the Standard of Christ in a new way, here are some ways to proceed. This chapter will give you some specific ways in which you, as presenter, can promote a Christ-centered supervision session.

Maintain Confidentiality

You've heard it before, but to reiterate, maintaining Christ-centered values requires that you to keep all aspects of a supervision session confidential. This protects you, your directee, and your supervision program. Never forget, each member of a supervision group is missioned with the task to keep confidential every part of a supervision session. In summary:

a. Consider <u>everything</u> you share about your directee to be confidential.

b. Don't discuss any part of a session with anyone outside of the supervision session, including team members, unless needed for further understanding, training, mental health concerns, or another clinical reasons.

c. Remind yourself before you present any supervision session that the session is confidential and focused on you, the presenter. It is human nature to drift into problem-solving or analyzing others. To stay focused on you, avoid answering

questions about the directee. This includes facts about his or her life, spirituality, reasoning, solutions, and any other aspect of life that could arise in supervision. If asked about a directee, you can respond with: "I'd rather not discuss my directee. Let's stay focused on me."
d. Don't forget to use a fake name for your directee and change details. Avoid connecting the identity of any directee to your supervision session, especially if others know who you are directing.
e. Discuss **your own** thoughts, feelings, responses or reactions. Perhaps you've been taught that focusing on yourself, your desires, needs or feelings is self-centered. Perhaps you feel emotionally safer if you discuss issues or people outside of yourself. Decide to trust your peers each time you present, then take the chance to share your deeper self.
f. Review Chapter 2 on Confidentiality if needed.

Trust God to Direct the Supervision Session

A supervision group of peers must pray together and separately. When you pray, you put the supervision session in God's hands. Prayers are built into the template for supervision meeting. Don't skip them.

At the beginning of every supervision session, pray that all peer group members will be open and Christ-centered during your session. Ask for the grace to set aside any thoughts you might have of riches, pride, and honor – even those connected to personality, knowledge, superiority, or saving face. Embrace poverty of spirit, humility and humiliation in your own heart and in the group. Trust that God will provide you with the insights you need, when you need them.

Be Perceptive

Everyone is exposed to a mountain of information every moment of every day. To survive this barrage of information overload, every person must ignore a multitude of sensory input including facts, attitudes and experiences that they experience throughout every day. For instance, you might not remember what you had for breakfast, which arm you slid first into your clothing, or how many bites of food you made during breakfast this morning, unless you broke your arm, have a tooth ache, or didn't get enough (or any) breakfast. According to authors Adler and Proctor in their book, **Looking Out Looking In,** several factors drive what a person chooses to notice.[44] These include:

- Intensity (brighter, bigger, more fun or irritating)
- Change (this is different than usual!)
- Motivation (I have a goal and notice whatever will get me there)
- Repetition (Something keeps happening and I want change)
- Preconceptions (Something is different than what I imagined or thought it would be.)
- Scatomas or Blind spots – (I don't notice that)

You are encouraged to evaluate each moment of the supervision session to decide what to say and when to say it. What do you notice about yourself or your peers? What will you ignore or dismiss? What's most important, noteworthy, or intense? What do you hear again and again? This is no easy task. It takes thought and attention to notice. Go into every supervision session with the intention of noticing where God is acting in your life and in your supervision session.

During your supervision session, remember that each peer experiences life uniquely with a different reality from yours. Your job as presenter is to deepen your understanding of yourself and your perceptions about the situation, So rather than feel judged during a session, you can accept as helpful whatever another person observes about you or your spiritual direction session.

When you do this, supervision will open your heart and mind to what God wants you to notice, thus deepening your insights, observations, and understanding.

Be Empathetic

Your ability to perceive is enhanced by empathy. Of course, you will never know another's point of view completely. But you can empathize. According to the Miriam-Webster Dictionary, "...*empathy* involves actively sharing in the emotional experience of the other person."[45] Best-selling author Daniel Goleman believes that cultivating the natural tendency toward empathy is the essence of social intelligence."[46] He incorporates five essential elements of emotional intelligence (EQ):

- **Emotional self-awareness** — you recognize what you are feeling and understand how your moods impact others.
- **Self-regulation** — you control or redirect your emotions; anticipate consequences before acting on impulse.
- **Motivation** — you utilize emotional factors to achieve goals, enjoy the learning process and persevere in the face of obstacles.
- **Empathy** — you sense the emotions of others.
- **Social skills** — you manage relationships, inspire others and induce desired responses from them.

Because supervision is a holy, relational look into another's soul, empathy in every group member helps deepen the experience. To empathize, you are asked to step out of yourself and set aside any angst you have about the process so that you can be present to your team members. Ask yourself what it might be like for them to experience humiliation or poverty of spirit? Can you help your peers deepen their desire to understand your motivation and desire?

Can you stand outside of yourself and observe what you are saying or feeling? Try to listen deeply to your own inner values, needs, desires, feelings, and actions, to identify the Standard (God or Evil [World, Flesh, Devil] as defined by St. Ignatius Loyola.) Share what you see, regardless of whether it looks tidy, holy, happy, and comfortable, or messy, disappointing, vulgar, or uncomfortable. Let yourself FEEL and share what you feel. This will greatly assist yourself, the team, and the process.

Empathy goes both ways. The peer group member is not your "enemy," teacher, guru, or spiritual director. Sometimes the peer group member knows less about supervision and spiritual direction than you do. Be kind. Realize that each person is in the group to help not hinder you. Think the best of each person, don't assume that anyone is out to harm or disrupt you. Remember that humility is Christ-like. Embrace it.

Promote Wholeness

You as spiritual director are much more than how you act or speak in spiritual direction. Because you love God, all things work together for good. Thus, God will use your talents and skills, faults and failures, attachments, and graces for good in your spiritual direction sessions. Allow all of you – the whole you – to enter supervision. Let your supervisors see your skills and talents, as well as faults and failures so they can help you integrate your attributes to develop a greater wholeness.

To promote wholeness, here are some questions you can ask yourself:

- What graces did I receive during the spiritual direction session that helped me in ways I didn't expect?
- Did I receive any unexpected, Godly thoughts or words that I used to respond to my directee?
- How did I use my gifts, and what aspect of my personality or life affected the spiritual direction session?

Be Transparent

As discussed earlier, whether the supervision process is helpful or destructive to the participants is dependent upon the supervision community's atmosphere. You already know that a supervision atmosphere must instill trust, caring, and love into every member, and group members' attitudes can have a great influence on others, especially the presenter, as to how open, honest, free, and Christ-like a person is.

What does transparency in supervision mean? I suggest it means each team member allows the other team members to see within his or her soul. The more clearly you communicate, give receptive feedback with openness and risk vulnerability, humility, even humiliation at times to get to the truth, the more transparent you become. Others (including God) will be more readily able to see into your heart and soul. To be effectively supervised, the windows and doors of your soul need to be transparent, or at least trying to be.

This is not always comfortable, of course. For transparency to occur, you must first know yourself well enough to know your affect and the Standard you are choosing . Then, you must trust

God enough to give your self-esteem and self-worth to Him. When you don't have to protect your own ego, you will be free to allow others to discover who you are, what you think and feel, and why.

Risk Honesty

Although your supervisory team members are responsible for creating the right environment to help the presenter be open and humble, you as presenter will have a better experience if you can admit mistakes, deficiencies, or attachments, while trusting that your group loves and accepts you as you are.

The Bible tells us that all Truth comes from God Who makes honesty possible. Truth then, creates a Standard by which to judge any action or statement. As mentioned above, honesty takes effort and risk. To develop honesty, learn what Truth is, and be willing to speak it with love. Read Sacred Scripture, talk with others, and learn more about your faith to deepen your understanding of God's Truth. Although media and culture may tell us that truth is relative and there is no absolute Truth, God says otherwise. In the Bible we read:

Luke 12:2 Everything that is now covered will be uncovered, and everything now hidden will be made clear.[46]

John 8:32 You will learn the truth and the truth will set you free.[47]

You as presenter are called to be honest with yourself, with God, and in the supervision session. For many people, this takes practice.

- Pray that God can help you set aside your fears of humiliation or confusion.

- Stop to listen to God's call to honesty. It could be masked by the fears of ridicule, self-disclosure, or vulnerability.
- Trust that God will assist you as you call to mind the aspects of your spiritual direction and your responses that need to be discussed.
- Choose to trust others. Even if members of your group act in ways that feel hurtful, realize you can choose your own emotion by returning to God's standard.
- Embrace the truth and God's Standard that includes poverty of spirit, humiliation, the humility. This will bring you closer to God and will greatly enhance the supervision session.

Listen Actively

Listening is more complex than just sitting quietly while another person talks. According to authors Adler and Proctor, "…listening is a process that consists of five elements: hearing, attending, understanding, responding, and remembering."[48]

1. **Hearing** is the physiological aspect of listening. Sound waves hit your ear, and your brain picks them up.
2. **Attending** is psychological. You as supervision presenter can learn to be attentive to group members, and by doing so, you become attentive to what the Holy Spirit is saying through them. In turn, peers are called to attend to the presenter with interest and concern. Being attentive helps both speaker and listeners.
3. **Understanding** happens when a message makes sense to us. But what someone else says is not always straightforward. You can ensure you've heard the message correctly by summarizing and asking if you've got it right. This is especially important in supervision, where we try to help a person clarify their feelings and Standards.

4. **Responding** to a message means giving observable feedback. Research suggests that feedback is important to the speaker, even the peer group member who is speaking to you about your supervision verbatim. You want your team to be good listeners for you. And in return, you improve the process by being a good listener to what they have to say. Show attentiveness by non-verbal behaviors such as eye contact, nodding, displaying appropriate facial features, waiting until they finish before you speak. Once you respond, do so with love and kindness.
5. **Remembering** is the ability to recall information. Research shows that most people remember only about 50% of what they heard immediately after hearing it.[49] Two months later, that drops down to 25%. Over time, we recall just a small fraction of what we hear. This is why it is so important to take notes after (or during if you can) each spiritual direction session. Train yourself to remember what a person said that you want to address. Then return to that point when you get the opportunity.

Practice active listening, using all five points, every time you participate in supervision (and spiritual direction), either as a presenter or team member.

Several other issues impact listening. Your personality, culture, timing, or cadence of your verbal expression all add to the ability of the group members to attend to all five aspects of listening. Help them along as they try to do so.

Listening Exercises for the Peer Supervision Team

Here's an exercise to help you overcome certain myths about listening.

Take some time to recall when:

1. You heard someone speaking but didn't attend to it.
2. You attended to the message but forgot it almost immediately.
3. You attended to and remembered the message but didn't understand completely.
4. You understood the message but didn't respond well enough to convey your understanding to the speaker.
5. You failed to recall some or all an important message.

Practice following all five elements of active listening in as many conversations as possible. This can be done with your family, friends, or at your employment as well as in supervision. Active listening is a skill that can be developed.

Section III

Tools for Peer Supervisors

12 Christ-Centered Values for Group Members

As soon as a supervision group is formed, a relational climate begins to develop. If you practice positive communication, that climate will also be positive. Both verbal and non-verbal communication contribute to this climate. Members of your group should speak, think, and act that will foster Christ-Centered values and positive communication patterns and process.

How Peers Foster Christ-Centered Model

The Catechism of the Catholic Church says, "The Holy Spirit gives to certain of the faithful the gifts of wisdom, faith, and discernment for the sake of this common good which is prayer (***spiritual direction***). Men and women so endowed are true servants of the living tradition of prayer."[50] As mentioned often above, you participate in any supervision group, your job is to help foster a Christ-centered model. Here are ways to do so.

First and Foremost, Seek God

As a peer supervisor, you are given the opportunity to help the presenter explore his or her efforts in trying to accomplish the goal: directing the directee toward God. To do this, you must go beyond technique, feelings, and spiritual enlightenment. Help the presenting spiritual director focus on God by asking where God was noticed. You can do this for yourself, first, by taking the time to see the speaker as if you are looking through Jesus' eyes. When you ask yourself how God might see the speaker, you bring your spirit under the Standard of Christ. This will also increase your respect for the speaker.

Pray before you speak. Try to calm your spirit as you pray before the session. Take time to consider each of these points:
- Depend on God for insight. Speak truth in love.
- Be honest and bold; tell the truth as you see it, even if it's hard. But do it with gentleness and kindness.
- Be transparent; admit your fears, biases, struggles, judgements.
- Promote wholeness; actively listen; be attentive to the other group members and the Holy Spirit.
- Challenge. Risk honesty, question suppositions.

Maintain Confidentiality

Reread chapter 2 on Confidentiality if needed. As mentioned there, to maintain Christ-centered values keep all aspects of a supervision session confidential. In summary:

g. Consider everything that anyone shares in supervision to be confidential.
h. Don't discuss any part of a session with anyone outside of the supervision session unless needed for clinical reasons.
i. Clarify the confidential nature of supervision at the beginning of every session.
j. Use fake names. Change details.
k. Avoid asking about the directee.
l. Discuss your own thoughts, feelings, responses or reactions.

Notice and Mention the Mood of the Room

You can help increase the capacity for others to engage and confront their own ideas if you remain impartial. The job of peer supervisors is to help the presenter explore his or her own affectivity during a spiritual direction session. So, work on being neutral and open. Listen to what the presenter says.

Encourage affectivity exploration. Where were the times of hope or despair, fear or trust, anxiety or peace, encouragement or discouragement, comfort or discomfort, adequacy or inadequacy, confusion or clarity? Your job is to uncover the depth of the affect, and the reason it occurred (within the director or peer).

As a peer supervisor, you are missioned with the task of letting go of judgments, of course. But even more, you must listen to your tone of voice and other non-verbal messages including your body language and facial expression to ensure you are giving a message of acceptance and love. If you aren't sure how you come across, or notice that the presenter is looking defensive, mention what you see. Then assure the presenter that you are on the side of truth and love only. Give affirmation and hope. Express your love for the person.

Sometimes a peer member projects strength or even power such that the conversation feels like interrogation or judgement. If you should notice non-verbal messages and tone of voice that cause defensiveness or lack of cooperation, speak up. Mention what you see. Don't let one person's habit of speech disrupt or destroy the supervision peer group.

Learn and Practice Metacommunication

It is very important for every peer in supervision to learn a way of speaking called metacommunication, which is communicating about the communication. For example, should you experience another's tone as judgmental, you need to switch to metacommunication so others know. Do this with an "I message" so you are telling the truth. For example, your comment might go like this: "I felt judged when Joan asked me about my feelings just now. The tone of her voice seemed hard. I had to force myself to answer. Is this something in me that needs to be worked on, or do others experience this also?"

Metacommunication isn't for problems only. It is an important tool for reinforcing aspects of supervision that are going well. For example, you might notice that someone was exceptionally helpful in exploring a particular aspect of your presentation or asking a question that prompted deeper inquiry for you. In this case, you might say something like, "I really appreciated that question. It helped me deepen my understanding of the situation. Thank you."

Time your comments. If the conversation appears to veer away from Christ's Standard or to the directee, or it impacts your ability to stay present and calm, mention it immediately. Otherwise, it is also appropriate to save such observations for the end of the session.

Practice humility and openness

Don't assume you are right. Admit mistakes and reveal your humanity. Discuss what you think and feel without judgement. State your thoughts or opinions, and then ask others to explore them with you. As in the prior example, you might add something like this: "This is what I think; how does this sound to you?"

To foster a Christ-centered atmosphere, no one other than Jesus Christ should be considered the "guru" or expert. If you are the person in the group that everyone seems to turn to for answers, step back from the conversation and permit others to speak. Humility allows all group members to develop ability and self-awareness. If you find yourself pontificating, talking more than others, feeling 'right' or being asked for your opinion often, go out of your way to defer to others. You can say something like, "I've said a lot today. So, before I answer, I'd like to know what you think." Humility and openness are keys in supervision.

Listen effectively

You as peer group member have the responsibility of listening with Christ in mind. Sometimes, the best response a listener can give is simply full attention. You can prompt a person to speak more in two ways: 1) stay silent or give minimal response, or 2) give brief statements of encouragement. Both give the other a chance to collect thoughts and feel supported. A compliment or even a smile might result in a compliment returned and reduced stress. This in turn will improve the relational climate.

For example, Mary brought an issue about her over-involvement in the life of her directee to supervision.

Mary: "I don't want to be so concerned about the person I'm directing. But her issues even keep me awake at night. I'm so worried about her problems that I don't pay enough attention to my own."
Peer Team Member Jack: "Hmm." [silence]
Mary: "I feel responsible. Like I'm her mother, you know? But I'm not."
Jack: "Good observation." [compliment]
Mary: "What should I do?"
Jack (smiling): "This is a tough problem. I'm glad you brought it to supervision. What do you think you need to do?" [positive body language, active listening, compliment]
Mary: Well, I need to let go of this. I'm not sure how, but I think

I need to trust God more....[several seconds of silence] I think that's it. I'm not trusting Jesus to be the savior. But that's my solution, isn't it."

It takes discipline to stay away from brainstorming solutions or focusing on issues outside of the presenter. But you and your team members will benefit greatly from practicing these prompts with humility and openness.

Learn what listening methods don't work and avoid them, also. These include pseudo listening (pretending to listen), talking too much (hogging the conversation), listening selectively (hearing only what you want to hear), defensive listening (formulating a response as you listen), ambushing, (which promotes defensiveness in the other person), and insensitive listening (ignoring nonverbal cues).

Know yourself. There are many reasons that can cause you to listen poorly. These include, to name a few: message overload, preoccupation, rapid thought, sloth or not wanting to put in the effort, external noise, faulty assumptions, lack of perceived benefit, lack of training, and even hearing problems. If you recognize any of these before or during supervision, pray about how you can overcome them or ask for help from your team.

Summary

There are many benefits for the spiritual director and peer supervisors when a group fosters the Christ-Centered model. First, the process frees the spiritual director to recognize vulnerabilities and move beyond them. Second, it improves the ability to notice and concentrate on movements within the directee. And third, it enables the director to be more God-centered. All three work together to promote spiritual freedom in all participants so that each can follow Ignatius' directive to "leave the creator to act intimately with the creature, and the creature with its Creator and Lord."[51]

Compassion and empathy are important tools for good listening; using them will keep you focused on the Standard of Christ as you listen. Beyond those, there are several listening techniques that you can learn to help deepen your ability to listen effectively.

a) Love first, then listen. See the speaker as if you are looking through Jesus's eyes.
b) Talk less, listen more. Allow others to speak.
c) Switch to metacommunication when needed.
d) Look for key ideas rather than solutions.
e) Don't assume you know what the person will say before you hear it.
f) Prompt a person to speak with silence or brief statements of encouragement.
g) Ask open ended questions. (No closed questions where a person can give an answer of yes or no.)
h) Learn to paraphrase what you've heard and repeat it back to the speaker.
i) Avoid distractions.

Practice

To improve your metacommunication, take time out to practice it on your own or with your group.

13 Creating the Supervision Environment

When you join a peer supervision group, the group works together to create a community of caring and love. This is an attitude that you each must create. But there are actions you can take together to help the process to be smoother and easier. For starters, supervision is easier if everyone knows when it will happen, and who will be presenting. In other words, supervision works best if you have a schedule and keep it.

Take time at the beginning of each season or year to meet as a group for business and planning. During that time, your group will function best if you decide ahead how long each part of the supervision session should go and how often each person will be supervised. (Suggestion: new directors need supervision monthly or even after each spiritual direction session. Experienced directors should be supervised at least twice yearly.) Together group members also decide what happens if a person does not follow the set guidelines.

A chart or list that includes dates, times, places, who will present, and who will facilitate each supervision session is also extremely helpful. When every member of the group has this schedule, they will have information about who will facilitate, be supervised, where and when the meeting will be, and how long the meeting will last.

Facilitator Guidelines

It's a good idea to rotate facilitators for the supervision meetings so that each person gets a chance to facilitate. When you are scheduled to be the facilitator, there are some steps you can follow to help make the process easier.

- Follow the supervision meeting agenda, especially the timing. This will help your group members feel more comfortable with the process and honor their time. (See Appendix for a sample agenda).
- Open and close the meeting with prayer. This can be verbal or silent.
- Remind other group members of your focus at the start of the meeting: on the presenter, not the directee.
- Reiterate at the beginning of every meeting that anything said by the presenter or the peer members is confidential, and should not be talked about anywhere outside of the meeting.
- Moderate the discussion as needed to ensure any discussion follows the intent, tone, and attitude described in this book. This means you encourage peers to treat each other with kindness and Christ-centered love, and you stop the group from any discussion on the directee's life or issues. Do not be afraid to interrupt the speaker, gently reminding that the conversation is about the presenter, not the directee. You can say words such as, "We are getting off-track here, focusing too much on the directee (or problem-solving). Let's come back to our presenter."
- Should the conversation veer toward solutions or methods needed for spiritual direction, either return the discussion to the affectivity of the presenter or announce that the conversation is going into consultation.
- Remain open to the Holy Spirit and assume the best about the presenter.

Group Focus

The person being supervised will have already chosen what they hope to explore with the supervisory peers. You as a member of that peer group should pay close attention to that statement, because it is the key to effective supervision.

As a supervisory peer group member, your job is to learn to listen to the unspoken and unrecognized values, judgements, and needs of the supervised spiritual director. Help that person develop insight and self-awareness and understanding of where a feeling comes from, **within that person**.

It's human nature to want to solve another's problems. Because it's often more fun and effective to talk about solutions than issues, any supervision conversation can easily drift toward brainstorming ways to make things better, or how the director might council the directee to solve a particular problem.

You as peer group member are missioned with the objective of being vigilant. Notice when the group veers off-track and remind everyone to come back to the subject – the presenter. Ask the presenter to clarify affect (his or her own affect, not that of the directee.)

The presenter or a peer can often get to affectivity by asking the question, "What, IN ME (or you, if asking the presenter), generated the feeling?

To reiterate, this is not about what the directee said or did. It's not about what is right or wrong. It's about what's happening in the heart and mind of the spiritual director. What's the internal self-talk, beliefs, values, and needs?

This is not easy to notice, nor is it natural for most people. But it is vitally important that every member of the supervisory peer group learn how to do this. It is helpful for you as peer member to practice this every time you participate in supervision. Stay vigilant, so you help the other team members focus on the presenter, and on internal, personal affectivity.

An example might help explain this more clearly.

Recently, our peer group met with a spiritual director named Grace. Here is what she listed as her intent.

"I want supervision before I meet my directee. I need to know how to proceed," she said, "but I'm really irked at having to meet with this person who rarely prays. She seems to spend most of her time obsessing about evaluating which man she should marry (she has two beaus) instead of where God is in her life. I'm tempted to 'fire' her, just end the relationship."

My Affect: I notice that Grace is very focused on the actions of her directee. I wonder why. She mentions one feeling, irked, so I bring that to her attention.

"Tell me about being irked," I say.

"Well, it seems like this person is taking advantage of me, not respecting the effort it takes to prepare for our sessions or the time I spend getting to and from them. She's hardly praying, and she cancels on a whim, expecting me to be ready when she is."

My Affect: I'm intrigued that Grace does not notice her own motivation for her feelings. I can hear her frustration.

"Tell me about you," I reply. "Why do her actions cause you to feel irked?"

Grace seemed confused. "Well, wouldn't that irk everyone?"

My Affect: It is easy to justify a feeling by saying everyone else would feel the same. But I know there's more. I want Grace to identify for herself why she is feeling irked in this case. I clarify why I'm being so obstinate in this line of questioning. (I want her to feel cared for not grilled. I want her to know that I want the best for her, even in my inquiries.)

"I'd say every person would have their own personal response to such an experience. So, we tell our retreatants that feelings come from within a person; they are not from someone else or from any experience. Can you identify where your feeling might be coming from? What are you thinking and judging and valuing that generates this feeling of being irked?"

"This is hard! Ok, I'll try again." She thinks for a moment. "Up to now, I've been trying to accommodate her desires. I adjusted and changed my schedule when she asked. I gently nudged when she didn't pray. I thought I was doing a good thing, being so subtle. But now I see I messed up. I think I gave her the impression that prayer and spiritual direction are trivial, that my time is not as valuable as hers, and she can act as she likes."

My Affect: Hurray! We are getting closer to Grace's heart. I'm feeling grateful for her perseverance and for the gifts God is giving us right now to hear the Holy Spirit.

"Sounds like you're saying you are irked that she isn't respecting your unnamed and unspoken boundaries." I say.

My Affect: I want to make sure I'm interpreting what she said correctly, so I paraphrase and say what I think I heard. I feel grateful again for the tools I have been given to help me do this.

"Yes, I guess I am. That's a good way to put it. And I'm irked at myself for not letting her know what my boundaries are. I need to tell her, so my emotions won't interfere with my peace and God's message when we meet… I feel freer."

My Affect: *She has located the internal reason for her feelings. I feel glad for this understanding.*

Through this process, Grace learned that when she ascribed her feelings to the actions of the directee, she felt helpless. Once she understood that the feelings came from within herself, and she was irritated with herself for not setting boundaries, she understood the problem and how to proceed. It freed her.

Stay open and attentive to the Spirit

Your ideas and thoughts about what to say to your directee requires insight and prayer. You are missioned to stay attentive to the Holy Spirit throughout every session. You can do this by focusing on the Standard of Christ in every word you speak. Choose your words carefully. There are ways to promote positive patterns of communication. You are missioned to listen to the Holy Spirit and keep the sessions productive.

Most likely, you already recognize the modes of speaking that you should avoid since they take a conversation in the wrong direction: away from God and into frustration, or that diminish the spiritual direction relationship. But to be clear, here's a list of a few that are not healthy ways of communication.

Complaint – counter complaint. A. "I wish you weren't so critical." B. "Well, I wish you weren't so negative."

Disagreement – disagreement. A. "Don't get down on me." B. "You're paranoid."
Mutual indifference – A. "I'm feeling blah, like I just don't care about life." B. "It must be in the water. I feel the same way."
Arguments involving questions. Q. "How can I talk when you won't listen? A: "How can I listen when you won't talk?"

Don't Protect

As peer supervisor or presenter, you are missioned to set aside parental, familial, friend-based methods of interacting that have been imposed upon you from birth by the culture you live in. One way to do this is to avoid emotional protection of others. It could be a norm in your culture for the kind protector to shield the person judged to be underdog, from inquiry negative feelings, or emotions. These, however, are important aspects of supervision. In supervision, refrain from protecting, shielding, or hiding emotions. You are not the savior of anyone.

If you feel tempted to protect another person in the group because you recognize his or her (or your) discomfort, switch your focus. Listen and comment on what you notice about yourself and your own affectivity. Why are you so concerned about protecting another's emotional well-being? What motivates you to try and protect someone or avoid conflict? Deepen your understanding of the values and needs that cause you to want to protect.

If you think another team member is being "picked on' or being asking questions that you judge to be too revelatory or adversarial, say so. You might ask the presenter something like: "This question seems too invasive to me. What's it like for you? Can you tell us what you are feeling right now?"

- Listen carefully to what the presenter has written or says, and the feelings he/she expresses.
- Take notes as the presenter speaks if this helps you remember. Alternately, you can write a summary or relevant section of the conversation after each session.
- Challenge the presenter to go deeper, encourage exploration of feelings – places where the director may have felt God's presence, places where he or she felt an impediment to God's presence.
- Keep the meeting focused on Christ-centered actions and attitudes.

Supervision Focus

During supervision, stay focused on the **presenter**. It is often tempting, when a group first begins, to get sidetracked toward the issues of the directee: his or her spiritual growth, the problem presented, how s/he might approach that issue, etc. Don't allow the conversation to veer in that direction.

All conversation about the directee, unless it's a serious problem that needs intervention or professional help, should be consciously avoided during a supervision session. It is the job of not only the facilitator, but also of every supervision group member to call the group back to supervision should the conversation stray to the directee or any other subject outside of the presenter and his or her feelings.

Several years ago, I was directing a woman whose life was scattered. This showed in her housekeeping – her home was always cluttered and dirty. At the time, I was reading a book about how to keep my home tidy, and I was tempted to tell her what I had learned. The urge was strong, and I had to stop myself many times from giving her advice. When I brought that to supervision, my team helped me realize that I would not be helping her spiritual turmoil by giving her instructions on her housekeeping. They stayed focused on me, the director, and helped me realize that my desire was a way in which I could feel "helpful."

Even after many years of supervision practice, group members can veer from focusing on the director to discussing the directee. Don't let that happen to your sessions. Stay focused on the presenter.

Practice supervision.

Follow the process in the outline, found in the Appendix, and do your best to act and speak within the Christ-centered model in both speaking and listening. Your group will improve over time. The greater the trust between members of the group, the better supervision will be.

14   Communication in Christ

As mentioned above, when we feel loved, we are more open to risk. If we know others care about us, we trust more. So, your main job as supervisory peer group member is to love each peer team member with the love of Christ. Of course this is no easy task. But you can begin by consciously recalling and embracing the Standard of Christ for yourself before every meeting. Then, you can contribute to a Christ-centered supervision environment by learning and using good communication skills.

Affirmation

In every supervision session, your job as peer is to affirm and assist the presenter to deepen self-evaluation while maintaining a Christ-centered attitude. This does not mean you agree with every question or comment that others make. It does mean, however, that you learn to ask questions in a non-threatening way so you do not interrogate, denigrate, alienate, but instead invigorate and affirm the person being supervised.

It is true that some communication methods and questions feel confrontational to some people but not others. So, you as peer group member are commissioned to closely observe the supervisee before and during the supervision session. Use your spiritual direction observational skills to evaluate the supervisee. Notice any nonverbal communication. According to Ronald Adler and Russel Proctor in their book on communication, **Looking Out Looking In,** verbal communication includes spoken words and written words. Nonverbal communication can be both vocal and non-vocal. Vocal non-verbal communication includes vocal tone, rate, pitch, volume, clearing the throat, stuttering, etc. Non-vocal communication includes gestures, movement, appearance, facial expression, touch, personal distance, eye contact, etc. Your job as supervisor is to notice all of these and evaluate the body language of the person being supervised.

The book goes on to say that all behavior has communicative value. "This impossibility of not communicating is extremely important to understand because it means that each of us is a kind of transmitter that cannot be shut off. No matter what we do, we give off information about ourselves." [52]

You can start every supervision session with some positive affirmation. This can be general, such as, "We are your friends and don't want to interrogate you." Or you can notice something specific in the presentation that you saw as positive.

Try to help the presenter view the process of supervision for what it is: a move toward God rather than an examination that must be passed; a deeper dive into the pool of grace rather than a cold shower of reality.

Clarification

Once you affirm your care for the person in the session, you might continue by describing the body language you observe, then asking what it means. "I see you looking down and fidgeting with your pen. Perhaps you're nervous? Can you tell us what's going on in you?"
This way, you take the unspoken affect out of the dark and put it in the light for all to explore. Sometimes, the supervisee is too concerned about being under scrutiny to relax, especially in the beginning of their career. This is not helpful to supervision,

because a person who is nervous or self-protective is not open to ideas or suggestions. Thus, the supervision is not effective. **Illustrate** what you infer by using observable data. For example, you might say, "I noticed that when you talked about this moment, you looked down at your hands and squeezed your eyes shut. From that I assume you are feeling nervous. Is that what was happening? Tell me more about what you feel."

Express reasons in a public, clear, and precise way. Describe how you got to the conclusions that you draw; ask others to look at the process with you. This not only helps you deepen your understanding, but also ensures that others understand your intention. For example, "I can see tears in your eyes, and you speak with force. Your conviction about God being in this session seems so evident. How was that for you?"

Seek contradictions and alternative explanations. You're trying to get at the truth or the best choice available. Ask for ideas that disagree with your own. "Here's what I think and feel. What other opinions do others hold?"

Ask others about their experience. For instance, if you notice that others stop talking after you speak your opinion, you might say something like, "Does my position in the group – or my forceful or nice way of speaking – make it hard to speak openly?"

Trust that the members in your group understand themselves, are listening to God, and want to be open. When you trust another, it's easier to take risks in what you share. It's easier to be open about yourself. Each person in the supervisory group is encouraged to work toward open, vulnerable communication. All participants benefit from transparency, and group members need to encourage others to work toward transparency. When all are risking, all share a deeper bond and confidentiality.

Work through blocks or hurdles. When people can't agree, keep talking so the group can come to some agreement. Let the group develop ways to test itself. "What can we do to find out if such-and-such is the case or not? How can we test out these competing values?"

Quieting Demands

In her book, ***Radical Optimism, Beatrice Bruteau*** writes: "We are to behold the beauty of the Lord, and it is the silencing of our distractions and private demands on life that makes this possible.... We can be peaceful, even in the midst of the demands of contemporary life, because what is really pressuring us is the insistence of our own demands....desires for approval and admiration, desires to be preferred and advanced, to succeed, to have power and wealth, to dominate others, to have things go our way, not to be inconvenienced or humiliated, desires to have the last word, to defend ourselves, to think well of ourselves, or even, perversely, to think ill of ourselves. All these desires which ordinarily cry out all day long to be heard and answered, all must be quieted."[53]

We do this through prayer, humility, humiliation, and through supervision that is honest and real, and focused on Christ.

Most people don't have good listening skills. We haven't been taught how to listen with our heart. Listening skills are so important in communication that the next chapter is devoted to them.

Focus on God

As noted before, one your main tasks as supervisor is to help all members of the group to stay focused on God, the presenter and affectivity throughout any and every session. So it is not just good, but appropriate in supervision to notice any conversation that drifts toward external events or the life of a directee, and with kindness, redirect to the presenter's affect and prayer. Also redirect any conversation on minutiae not related to the supervision process or Standards. In this way you help guarantee a good supervision session for all.

Here are some statements that you can use to help your supervision sessions stay on track.

- Yes, those issues do impact your directee's life greatly, and I can see that you want to help. But we aren't here to solve problems. Can you tell us more about your affectivity relating to this issue?"
- We have strayed. We are talking too much about the directee, and his/her life. Let's return to the spiritual director and supervision.
- I feel uncomfortable with the direction of this conversation. Let's get back to supervision.
- Can you say more about where you find God in what you are discussing?
- We have drifted off into consultation. Let's decide if this is where we should be. Or do we return to supervision until we have a clearer understanding of what needs to be addressed?

Listen to Body Language

As you proceed into supervision, you might identify a feeling or notice specific body language in the presenter. Do not be afraid to ask for deeper evaluation of that feeling.

For example, during one supervision session, the presenter kept clenching his fist when he discussed a conversation he had with his directee. One supervisor said, "Tell me about that tight fist. What are you feeling?" He stared at it, as if it belonged to someone else. "I didn't even know I was doing that," he said. He spent a few moments considering it. "Huh! I didn't realize it, but I'm angry about this situation."

The next chapter will develop listening more deeply.

Questions

What impedes or helps you to keep focus on yourself during supervision?

If you have trouble keeping your directee focused on prayer and God, or if you realize your directee often veers from the spiritual to just chatting, then this is a good subject to bring to supervision.

15 Listening with Heart

For a peer supervisor to gain a complete picture of someone's communication, listening must involve more than just the ears. Active listening requires that the listener say little so that the speaker can fully explain the subject. Impressions or assumptions do not give a clear enough picture of the speaker's intent.

A good listener spends time learning and practicing the five steps mentioned above, listed here in summary.

> **Hearing** - physiological aspect of listening.
> **Attending** to the Holy Spirit and speaker.
> **Understanding** and summarizing or asking for clarification.
> **Responding** – give observable feedback.
> **Remembering** - recall what was said.

If you want to be a good listener, here are some simple ways of acting that you can practice.

- Don't judge what was said or wonder whether it is correct or not.
- No need to contemplate your response as you listen. Instead, think about what you are hearing and trust that God will help you know what to say when it's time for you to speak.
- Engage your mind, spirit, and all five senses so that you hear beyond the words, to the emotions of the speaker. You will be a good listener if you notice body language and ask about it.
- Don't assume you know what the person meant by what was said. Clarify.

Summarize as you listen. Say what you think you've heard and give the speaker the opportunity to correct or affirm your evaluation. According to psychologist Jordan Peterson, the act of summary aids the person in consolidation and utility of memory. With summary, the memory gets better. It is distilled and the "moral of the story" is extracted. So that what could be a rant becomes, 'This is what happened. This is why. This is what I must do to avoid such things from now on.' That's a successful memory. You remember the past not so that it is 'accurately recorded,' or to say it again, but so that you can be prepared for the future."[54]

Summarize your directee's conversation so you put into succinct words what your directee said in many words. You will also have a synopsis of the conversation for your supervision paper.

Carl Rogers wrote this about listening. "The great majority of us cannot listen; we find ourselves compelled to evaluate, because listening is too dangerous. The first requirement is courage, and we do not always have it. ... The risk of being changed is one of the most frightening prospects most of us can face." [55]

Listening can be frightening or even dangerous because it can transform people – and that includes both you as listener and speaker. Supervision then becomes a deep dive into self, and a deep exploration of some dangerous and frightening places – the heart and soul. We should not go to those places without the help of the Holy Spirit.

In his book, *12 Rules for Life, and Antidote for Chaos,* author Jordan Peterson writes, "There are several primary advantages to this process of summary. The first advantage is I genuinely come to understand what the person is saying."[56]

Bodily Changes with Emotion

When someone experiences strong emotions, many bodily changes occur. Research mentions changed heart rate, changes in appearance such as sweating, fidgeting, blushing, blinking, etc. Other changes include tone of voice, gestures, posture, facial expression, and more. Although you might easily notice these changes in another, interpreting them correctly is not as easy. Non-verbal communication can be ambiguous, confusing, or downright deceiving. This makes your job as peer supervisor challenging, but there are tools you can practice that help clarify the meaning of those non-verbal actions.

To clarify your observation, ask the other what those bodily changes mean. For instance, looking down could mean embarrassment, or the person is taking a moment to think, or even is not willing to say and is shutting down. A smile could be happiness or nervousness, or a way to cover anger. Tears could be from joy or sorrow, frustration, or more. You won't know what prompts those bodily changes until you ask.

Learning to read bodily cues helps you to "listen" fully. A spiritual director once told me during supervision that she was feeling okay, yet she looked nervous and distracted. I mentioned to her what I was noticing in her body language. That's when she poured out her stress about how a serious family matter impacted her spiritual direction session. The session turned from mundane to very helpful for her.

Most people notice body language in others. Now you can hone your understanding of such language and help your peers do so also.

Summarize

Confirm your conclusions or thoughts by summarizing what you heard. When someone else is speaking, explore his or her thoughts completely and feelings before adding yours. Use active listening techniques. Say things like, "When you say that, I think you mean _____ (fill in blank). Is that right?" Or, "I heard you say _____. Is that what you meant?"

This process will teach you how to listen to the whole person with an open mind and hear what that person is trying to express.

Perception

One important aspect of supervision is attitude. You can help the presenter feel comfortable enough in the group to be open and willing to share from the heart, even at the first meeting. To set the correct mood, start with prayer and commit to looking for God throughout the supervision session.

As mentioned earlier, at every moment, each of us is exposed to so many stimuli that it is impossible to notice everything. Thus, every human being continually sorts information, and focuses it through a personal lens. Observation is deeply affected by the lens of attitudes, beliefs, values, and more that the perceiver uses to view the world. As a result, no two people see a situation in the same way.

This was highlighted for me when, for my father's 80th birthday, each of my siblings wrote a memory of growing up on the family farm. My biologist sister remembered the flowers and garden, my engineering brother remembered repairing machines, while my veterinarian brother recalled caring for the animals. Each looked at childhood through the lens of his or her interests.

Besides interests, many other factors influence our perception of a situation. Low or high self-esteem can cause a person to judge self either more rigidly or more charitably than others. One person might cling to first impressions and can't see another beyond them while another waits to make an evaluation.

Recently, one of our interns, Zoe, presented her first supervision paper. Our group spanned two states and four cities, so we met over Zoom. At the end of the session, Zoe said she thought we were too tough on her. She wanted more affirmation. I felt surprised by her comment and thrilled that she could voice her need and affect. When she said this, I realized that we, the seasoned spiritual directors, had indeed made the mistake of treating her like a veteran spiritual director. Only her face was visible on Zoom so we didn't get the body-language normal cues about her discomfort. Fortunately, she was self-aware enough to let us know.

Your group can diminish stress for new spiritual directors in several ways. First, notice body language if possible. If the person looks nervous, address that when you see it. If your group meets online, be more conscientious and ask about participant affect often, especially if you notice a sign of stress or if you have new members of the group.

Use the sandwich technique. Start with affirmation. Review the supervision paper and highlight the positive aspects that you can mention before you get to anything else. Sandwich in the content that could be challenging for the person to hear. Then end with more positive affirmations.

Self-Love

In supervision, you as peer group member are called to continually work to love yourself and others the way God does. According to St. Ignatius, this is the foundation of the Spiritual Exercises and of spiritual growth: Love yourself as God loves you. When this type of self-love increases, humility and humiliation become easier, and even embraced. These are the fruits of the Standard of Christ; they lead us to deeper growth and love.

Self-Evaluation

While you listen with attention in supervision, notice how you are responding to what is being said. What do you see, hear, taste, feel, smell? What do you feel – tension, hope, energy, sorrow? Return to the circle of feelings (pg. 68 above) and find one or two that clearly define how you are feeling. What values do you hold that cause you to feel as you do?

Regularly evaluate your strengths and weaknesses. This deepens honesty, which is vital for those who are presenting and those who are supervising.

Develop humility, humiliation and poverty of spirit. These are vital attributes for any supervisor.

Trust God

Trust God rather than your assumptions, impressions, or judgements. Every person has positive and negative traits; every person is deeper than any of us know. You, as peer supervisor, are called to view each person with love and grace.

Don't assume you fully understand what anyone else is feeling, thinking, or evaluating. Your interpretations are not theirs. It is human nature to analyze and try to make sense of the other's comments or motives. But it is vital that you don't assume you've got the "right" answer. Once you've analyzed, work to confirm, paraphrase, and clarify before you advise or comment. You want to understand the presenter.

Learn to check your perception, using these three steps.

1. Describe the behavior you notice.
2. List two or more possible interpretations of the behavior.
3. Request clarification about how to interpret the behavior.

Here are a few examples:

"When you looked down at your hands and were quite for quite for a minute *(behavior),* I wasn't sure if you felt embarrassed and shut down *(first interpretation)* or were confused and praying about what to say next *(second interpretation).* Can you clarify for us? (*request for clarification*).

"I notice tears on your cheeks as you talked about that experience. *(Behavior)*. To me you look sad, *(first interpretation),* but your words suggest joy *(second interpretation).* Can you help us understand more about what you are feeling? *(request for clarification.)*

Selecting

Supervision works best when all peers, including the presenter, understand why a particular session was chosen for supervision. You, as peer supervisor, should understand why and how you are selecting what you talk about during supervision. To do so, consider what you notice and why. You might notice a comment or reaction because it is more intense or different than before.

If I am running late, for instance, I might notice the time more. If you are dealing with your own strong affect (how something in my life affects you), you might not want to address strong affect in another. Or perhaps you recognize some big change or repetition of actions that seem troublesome (noticeably repetitious). Almost anything can motivate your selecting a subject or affect to discuss during supervision. If you pay attention to your motives, you can more easily select the affect or action that God calls you to notice and select for discussion. [57]

Interpreting

Once you have perceived and understood what the presenter wants to express or you discover the session's intent, it is your job as peer supervisor to help the presenter interpret, that is, attach meaning to, the data. In this case, you will interpret the information you hear in supervision, as well as what you notice in the presenter – body language and such. Several factors affect how we interpret an event:

    a) Degree of involvement with the other person
    b) Personal experience
    c) Assumptions about human behavior
    d) Attitudes & expectations
    e) Knowledge
    f) Self-concept
    g) Relational satisfaction [58]

Our personal insecurities, assumptions, and attitudes make a big difference in how we interpret information. We might judge a behavior to be positive when we are pleased with someone but complain about that same behavior when we aren't pleased. As we move into supervision, all of this comes to the forefront of our actions and thoughts about what we say and how we say it.

Questions

Asking questions is a common way to get information from people. Questions have been called the "most popular piece of language"[59] because the answers fill in facts and details that help understanding. However, not all questions are equally helpful. It is the responsibility of every peer supervisor to learn how to ask questions appropriately such that the presenter is not intimidated, dismayed, or stumped by them.

First, let's look at problems with questions.

Closed questions, ones that require a yes or no answer, are not useful in supervision or in spiritual direction.

Counterfeit questions are aimed at sending a message, not receiving one. Many counterfeit questions are also closed questions. Consider removing questions of the types listed below from your asking repertoire[60]:

- Questions that make statements. A question such as: "You haven't been praying, have you?" traps the presenter. Instead you might say, "Tell me about your prayer life."
- Questions that end in a 'tag' such as 'did you?', 'would you?', 'isn't that right?' Also, questions that start with 'Don't you…' or 'do you…' are problematic questions. For example, if you ask, "Don't you think you were a bit harsh with her?" gives the presenter no option but to counter you or agree.
- Questions that hold hidden agendas. For example, "Were you praying through that experience?" is problematic. Instead

you might ask, "What was happening inside of you during that experience?

- Questions that seek 'correct' answers. For example, "You've been praying daily, I assume?" is not as effective as, "Tell me about your prayer schedule."
- Questions based on assumptions or conclusions. Questions such as "What's wrong?" "Why are you upset?" assume that there is some issue. "Why aren't you listening to me?" assumes the other person is not paying attention. Clarify if your assumption is correct before you ask about the conclusion. For instance, you might ask, "You look uncomfortable (or distracted or unhappy). Can you tell me what you are thinking or feeling?"

These types of questions above impede you from getting the information you need for effective spiritual direction and supervision.

Open-ended, sincere questions or statements, on the other hand, can be very helpful. Every peer member should focus on questions that help the group and therefore the spiritual director gain information that will help the presenter.

Counterfeit Question Exercise

Your supervisory group can work together as a team to improve questions and responses. Assign one person to be the "presenter" and the others act as peer supervisors.

Assign one person as the "supervisor."
Other peers take turns being the "presenter."
- The Supervisor asks the first presenter question #1: Instead of answering the question, the "presenter" explores what affect was felt during the question. Then,

suggest a question that would be more useful.
- The next peer becomes the "presenter." The "supervisor" asks question #2. This presenter tells what affect was felt during the question, then suggests a question that would be more useful.
- Rotate through all peers until everyone has had a chance to comment on the questions and explain why they are not helpful and suggest a way to ask that would be useful.

1. "Did you start with a prayer?"
2. "You don't trust God, do you?"
3. "Were you praying through that experience?"
4. "What's the matter?"
5. You weren't listening, were you?
6. "I don't think you really meant that, did you?"

16 Issues You Might Discover

Questions

Some people do not respond well to **any** questions, even open, kind, or nonjudgmental questions. Perhaps questions were used by a person's family of origin or others to shame, blame, trap, or manipulate. But you, or even they might not know that.

When you as peer supervisor ask any question, notice the presenter's response. Do not let negative presenter responses or affectivity pass without investigation. If you detect resistance, animosity, or other negative response, mention what you see. Help the presenter uncover reactions, and the source of them, so the session runs smoothly and without communication issues.

Don't let someone's aversion to divulging deeper aspects of self or to questions disrupt or divert the process of supervision. If a member of your group can't answer questions without feeling judged or belittled, you as a group can address this issue in two ways.

First, name the issue. Point out to the presenter that he/she seems extra sensitive to questions. Discuss that sensitivity. If possible, help the presenter uncover any fear of judgement or ridicule from questions. Ask how the group might be able to get information in a way that would not cause distress.

Second, find ways to get information without asking. "Listen" beyond the words. Notice body language as well as the words someone speaks. Describe what you see, give options, provide at least two different reasons, and conclusion. Make statements based and ask for verification. Here's a more detailed instruction on how to do this.

Describe what you see in the presenter. You might define it as anxiety, nervousness, hesitancy. If you notice that the presenter looks uncomfortable in some way, address that discomfort before you address any other supervision topic. You might say something like, "Before we get into the subject you brought up, let's talk about what's going on inside of you right now. After I asked that question, you looked away and your lips tightened. *(observation.)* Did that question cause you a problem, *(first conclusion)* or are you trying to figure out an answer? *(second conclusion).* Can you tell us about your affect?"

Prayer

Your primary purpose as a spiritual director is to direct a person toward God. How well you do so is a function of how well you can notice when this is happening and how well you can direct your own self and prayer toward God. So, both peers and the presenter should be striving at every moment to be Christ-centered, to live under Christ's standard, while helping others to do the same.

You can request any presenter talk about prayer: "Tell us more about how you attended to your directee's prayer during this direction session." This can get the presenter thinking about the goal of spiritual direction, and if that goal was achieved in a particular conversation.

If you, as peer member, notice the presenter avoiding the experience of prayer, ask about it. For example, in one supervision session, the presenter, Maude, mentioned that she had trouble praying about sin when she made the Spiritual Exercises a few years ago. Now as spiritual director, she said, "That's ***private.*** I don't want her to feel uncomfortable or embarrassed." Maude hadn't heard any of those feelings from her directee, yet she projected her feelings of discomfort onto the directee. Why? As mentioned above, actions, life choices, circumstances of the **DIRECTEE** are considered private in supervision. The feelings of the supervision presenter that relate specifically to the supervision session are not. It is the job of the team to help the presenter understand what feelings arise, and why. That's the whole point of supervision.

You as supervisor might want to help someone like Maude discover why she is feeling such discomfort about the "possibility" of something being disclosed. What values, needs, and especially Standard within Maude elicited such a response? In such a situation, you as peer might ask:

- "What are your personal experiences of, and assumptions about sin and prayer?"
- "You seem to feel responsible for your directee's comfort. Tell us more about that."
- "Tell us about the discomfort you feel in talking about prayer in relation to sin.

When a presenter refuses to discuss affect relating to a spiritual direction or supervision session, switch to metacommunication and ask about that refusal. For example, if a presenter says certain feelings are 'private' you might ask, "What makes you label them private?" Or, "You seem embarrassed by your emotion. Can you explain that more?"

After exploration of any refusal of sharing in supervision, consultation can be used to help the presenter deepen self-awareness and personal freedom.

Grace

Another important aspect of spiritual direction is to assist the directee with asking for grace, and noticing when it has been received. This assumes that the spiritual director can notice such signs of grace. Here are some questions or thoughts that might help a presenter focus on grace:

- What is your understanding of grace and its importance to your directee and the spiritual direction session?
- Tell us about how you experienced God's grace during this session?
- How do you feel about giving your directee explicit graces to ask for or focus on? Why?
- What signs of grace (and which graces) did you experience in your directee during this session?
- What, during either the spiritual direction session or this supervision session, most helped or hindered your attentiveness to God and why?
- How are you attending to the graces that your directee is asking for during prayer time?
- Are there any aspects of grace that you'd like to discuss or expand on?

Strong Feelings Between Director and Directee

Any strong feelings that arise within a director due to the relationship with a directee should be processed in supervision. In her book, from each other, admiring some traits but disliking other traits in the other, and projecting feelings onto the other. When director and directee experience any relational dynamic that interferes with the direction encounter and the contemplative focus, they need to bring the dynamics of the relationship to supervision."

Some issues that could arise include: 1) directee or director falls in love with the other. 2) One feels strong sexual attraction to the other. 3) both notice friendship developing so the director needs to decide to continue directing or become a friend. 4) Director feels controlled by the directee. 5) director feels anger or helpless concerning actions or attitudes of the directee including manipulation, avoidance, sloth, passive aggression, or other.

Transference and counter-transference are common.

Transference

According to the website, A Very Well Mind,[61] The American Psychological Association (APA) defines transference as a process whereby one person projects his or her own conflicts onto another. For example,

Gloria, a spiritual director, brought to supervision a concern about her relationship with her directee, Madaline, who reminded her of her daughter. Gloria found herself slipping into mother mode with her directee. In supervision she asked for help to understand why she did, and how to stop doing so. At the end of the session, she realized that she was transferring her need to be important in her grown children's lives onto her directee.

Joseph came to supervision with a fear of his directee even though the man was polite and kind. Supervision helped him understand that his own issues at work with his boss were fueling a transference of feelings onto his directee.

Counter-Transference

The APA defines counter-transference as "a reaction by the director to the directee's transference." For example, the directee begins to idolize the director, complimenting, or sending cards or even gifts. If caught in counter-transference, the director might feel honored and important, and fail to accurately notice God working in the life of the directee.

There are four ways in which counter-transference occurs.

- The director's unresolved issues cause it.
- The director reacts to the directee's transference.
- The director is over-supportive, trying too hard to befriend the directee, and discloses too much.
- The director acts out against uncomfortable feelings in a negative way, including being overly critical and punishing or rejecting the directee.

Counter-transference is common, especially in novice spiritual directors, so you as supervisor need to pay close attention and help team members become more self-aware. You might not be able to eliminate counter-transference altogether. But you can assist the spiritual director to know how to use those feelings productively.

Any issue that threatens values, beliefs, or relational balance could prevent a director from being able to see the person with agape love or see the issue clearly. Both spiritual director and supervisor team member are missioned to 1.) Notice if any transference or countertransference is happening, and 2) Bring these issues into the light by discussing them. Some examples include:

- One feels strong sexual feelings for the other, or both feel a growing attraction toward the other.
- A directee begins to fall in love with the director, or vice versa.

- Both directee and director notice a friendship forming between them.
- A director feels controlled or dominated by the directee.
- A director experiences manipulation, passive-aggressive behavior, or other dysfunctional actions by the directee and feels angry or helpless about those experiences.
- A directee becomes afraid of deepening intimacy, or of the spiritual director's questions, or of the spiritual direction session itself, and resorts to blame or avoidance to escape self-revelation.
- A directee accuses the director of probing or pushing. The director in turn feels hurt or confused.

Here are some questions you can ask to help explore this:

- How do you see the relationship between you and your directee?
- You say you and your directee get along well. Can you identify what that means to you?
- You mention conflict relating to your directee. Can you take a moment to clarify this conflict? What do you think causes it and what is your emotional response?
- From what you say, there appears to be some sort of threat or challenge to your values, beliefs, or psychological adjustment in this relationship. How do you see that challenge in relation to the spiritual direction session?
- You mentioned that you've noticed issues of ... [dependency, attachment, sexuality, anger, power, or manipulation.] How do you interpret their presence in relationship to God and grace?

- At one point, you shared some of your own experience with your directee. How did that sharing modify the spiritual direction session or the relationship?
- You seem to enjoy (or dread) the company of your directee very much. How would you classify your relationship? What impact does that have on spiritual direction?

Both transference and countertransference are normal parts of relationships, but it is the spiritual director's job to recognize them and do what's necessary to remain neutral.

Self-Revelation

Your job as peer supervisor is important. You and your team are missioned with helping the presenter discover more about him- or herself. This is both a great honor and great responsibility. You'll want to notice the emotions and affectivity expressed by the presenter, of course. But why? Keep in mind that your job is to help uncover the standard under which the presenter stood that caused the feeling to arise. Since you are missioned to uncover which standard the presenter focused on during an emotional response, you yourself must remain under the Standard of Christ.

To reiterate, you will need to study and practice evaluating your affect relating to Christ's Standard.

Standard → Need → Value → Affect → Action

This is the process by which feelings (affect) arise. The standard creates a need, from which we form values, out of which come our feelings and then actions. To discover the Standard, your quest as supervisor is to work this process backwards, starting with action or affect. Once you identify your feeling, continue to explore which values you hold that are respected or not. Notice your needs met or not, then uncover what Standard those needs arose from. The better you learn how to do this, the more you can help presenters do it, also.

Besides identifying your Standard, you can also help the presenter in several other ways including growth in self-awareness, deepening awareness of God's presence in spiritual direction, and their ability to notice transference and counter-transference.

Some requests or questions that help a presenter focus on self include:

- How willing are you to look beyond the obvious to search for values and needs beneath feelings? Where did you do that in this spiritual direction session?
- What is the nature of your confidence or lack of it? What do you think about humility and humiliation?
- Tell us about your listening skills, your ability to focus, and/or your openness to change.
- Tell us what you were feeling when you said _____. Can you identify what values you hold that prompted that feeling?
- Please discuss the feeling you noted in your verbatim in paragraph _____ (name feeling such as discomfort, joy, enthusiasm, hope, discouragement, etc.).
- How did you address the personal issue you encountered?
- How do you feel about confronting issues that are humbling, or even humiliating?

Discernment

How did you see discernment happening in your spiritual direction session is very important. Every spiritual director would be wise to memorize the rules so that any time a directee uses a rule, even if they don't know it, you can point it out. Here are some questions you can ask the presenter about discernment.

- What rules for discernment did you use during your discussion? (See Chapter 10 for a list). Why?
- How did you address consolation (or desolation) in the directee?
- What would it be like for you to explain that rule of discernment to your directee right when it was needed?
- What's the difference for you between discernment and teaching or giving advice?
- It looks to me that your personal mood or spiritual affectivity influenced your directee and his discernment. Tell us about that.
- How do you understand the balance between relying on knowledge as opposed to radical openness to the Spirit?

17 Supervision Techniques

Along with learning to listen with intent, techniques like those you've learned and use in spiritual direction can be effective in supervision. These include mirroring, clarifying, affirming, and inviting or challenging depth. Here are just a few examples.

Mirroring

This technique involves listening skills that you will find in the prior chapter. Listen carefully to unspoken body language as well as words. Repeat what you heard, especially a person's affect, using different words. You can also use some of the same words you heard to show that you understood the basic content of what the person said and summarize.

It is the job of every supervisory team member to notice feelings and reactions in a presenter, call to attention to them, and ask for clarification. When and if you do, you can help keep your supervisory team focused on the Christ-centered model.

You might use this sentence to help you clarify what you heard. *"It sounds like you are feeling …."* Or, *"You say you are feeling …. Can you expand for us what that means to you?"*

In this example, the directee reported that God feels distant, not personal.

Directee: I don't think I've felt the presence of Jesus the way you describe. But I'm learning a lot. I usually just scan the stories. I know them all well.

Director affect: I feel thankful for his honesty but he is missing the beauty of relating to Jesus more personally. I want to do the best job that I can, and make sure he can deepen his relationship with God during his prayer time. I'm not feeling very confident. Does he recognize that; can he see the doubt I have in my own abilities? Am I the right person to direct him, I wonder?

Supervisor response: "You say you are thankful for honesty, but not confident in yourself. Can you expand on that?

Spiritual Director response: "I'm thankful that my retreatant is honest. That helps me to understand. I don't know how to get him from head knowledge of God to a deeper heart knowledge. I feel inept, clueless.

When a person hears their own words spoken back to them, they can consider what was said and deepen understanding. Use mirroring whenever you want to condense or affirm what's happening within the heart of the speaker.

On occasion, you may encounter an experience where a person responds negatively to the question or comment you've made. He or she might appear irritated by it, especially if you copy the other person's words exactly.

Clarifying

Listen carefully, then condense what the person said. Your job is to understand more clearly what he or she is feeling or thinking. Sometimes a person talks in broad strokes, weaving many words around the main point. Sometimes a person might jump back and forth to different subjects, grabbing bits and pieces of information to illustrate the point. Sometimes, a person may not even understand what the point of the conversation is. You, as supervisory team member can assist by listening carefully. Then, extract and express the main points you heard. Finally, in clarification, you ask if you heard correctly in your summary. Don't assume you know what the other person means.

Let the other team member tell you what he or she meant or felt. Use this or a sentence like it.

"I want to understand better, so let me summarize what I heard you say." OR *"So I think you are saying (fill in what you heard) ... Am I hearing you correctly?"*

Here's an example:

Spiritual director: "I feel helpless to assist my directee. She isn't praying and often cancels our appointments. I also don't want to waste my time setting up meetings that she doesn't come to. And her chatter is not meaningful or related to God. I feel tempted to tell her that I can't continue directing her if she doesn't pray and fails to show up for sessions. How do I know when I should do that, and when I should continue?"

Supervisor response: "So you are concerned that your directee is not doing the work, and want to know if you are being tempted or called to tell her you can no longer direct her, right?"

"Yes exactly. Now that you put it that way, it's clearer. On one hand, it is a temptation, because I want out of the situation. On the other hand, I see God calling me to step away and give her the chance to see consequences of her actions."

Clarifying her emotions helped the director sort out the decision.

Affirming

"Did you notice what happened there? I am impressed that you were able to...."

One of the most important spiritual direction skills that is also used in supervision is the affirmation. Get in the habit of using it often and with enthusiasm. This means you tell the person the positive aspects of what has been shared, and what you perceive she or he learned from that experience. This requires work on your part. You must look beyond the negative aspects of any action or feeling and discover the hidden beauty hiding there. Then, you must speak it for all team members, especially the presenter, to hear. In a book published in 1965, a Jesuit wrote, "Love looks for what is lovable and finds it." This is what we are called to do in our ministry, and make sure we affirm as much as possible.

Often, someone may not know if their insights or experiences are drawing them closer to God, or if these events are figments of the imagination. You and me and most everyone has been trained to focus on the negative, to notice variance and error. Our culture and human nature trains us to notice difficult issues, struggle, dissent, and sorrow. We learn to notice to avoid pain that these usually cause. Yet, we easily gloss over grace, enthusiasm, insight, and generosity, thus missing God's constant presence in life experiences. This might be self-preservation, but it isn't Christ-centered. You as supervisor are instead called to notice and affirm the positive. I challenge you to discover something positive in every situation.

One spiritual director had been meeting with her directee a few times when she came to supervision. The spiritual director finally asked the directee how long she was praying each day and the answer surprised and sobered her.

"I didn't realize my directee was spending so little time reflecting on what God is saying to her. Sometimes just a few minutes a day! She kept talking about how wonderful her prayer was, and how close to God she was. I think I knew something was amiss because it always seemed so great. There was no normal up and down. I don't know if she intentionally was trying to fool me, but I'm disappointed in myself for missing the signs."

Supervisor: "Good insight. You have come to realize that a directee can have wonderful words and a good way to convince you, that you are prone to believe.

"I guess you are right! Now that I know this, I will keep her focused on the task of prayer, and I won't be tricked by her fancy words. I think I will recognize when she strays, too. This is a great lesson."

Going Deeper

"It might be a good idea if you.... Have you pondered...?" Would you consider going back to that and praying about ...?

Your job as supervisor is to call the spiritual director into deeper connection and relationship with Christ so that awareness of God as the spiritual director increases. St. Ignatius talked of the 'magis' (the more) and when you invite a spiritual director to go deeper into their soul, you are helping that person grow in spirit.

As peer group member, you can best accomplish this by remaining prayerful during supervision. Listen carefully to how the supervised person might be draw closer to God. Ask the Lord if you should share your thoughts about that.

The spiritual director quoted her directee. "I feel such comfort and closeness with Jesus and Mary. It's deeply personal, like speaking with a friend. I don't do this as much with God the Father though. I mean, he's GOD. He has more important things to do than chat with me. He's GOD!"

Director affect: I am surprised. I thought the directee was so connected to God.

Director response: "You know God loves you, right?"

Team member response: "From that question, it looks to me that you assumed you knew how this person was thinking and feeling, but you didn't confirm that assumption with her. Tell us about what prevented you from clarifying with your directee her intent.

Director response: I thought I was using intuition and sensitivity to understand what the directee was saying. Now that you ask about it, I see that I wasn't. I assumed to know stuff that I couldn't know. I didn't ask about or hear the inner thoughts and feelings of my directee because I was sure I knew the answer…. Rather presumptuous of me. This is a bad habit I need to break.

Summary

These spiritual direction techniques of mirroring, clarifying, affirming and challenging a person to depth can be used during each supervision session to help supervised person move closer to Christ. Every one of them will help deepen understanding of what happened during the spiritual direction session, for you and for your directee both. Feel free to use them often.

Peer Supervision – Beyond the Basics

18   Dealing with Stress

We as Spiritual Directors choose to follow Jesus. He summons us as apostles to the highest spiritual poverty! Yipes. What a calling. Do you accept it? Can you spread the sacred teaching to the world? Are you willing to embrace spiritual or even actual poverty? Are you willing to choose insults and contempt? St. Ignatius reminds us that "from insults and contempt spring humility... So we learn that it is poverty, humility, and humiliation (or contempt) that leads us to all other virtues. (Spiritual Exercises 146).

Supervision often illuminates places where the presenter or even the peer group members are not following the Standard of Christ. This is one big reason we do supervision. It is designed to dig deeply into psychological, social, and spiritual areas of the presenter (aka the spiritual director). These areas are often off-limits in other social or familial conversations or discussions. Thus, you might have little practice dealing with such issues. Also, because supervision delves deeply into the human psyche, no matter how carefully a group sticks to the process and stays focused on the Standard of Christ, emotional stress or even distress can occur. There are ways in which you can address or mitigate this stress to assist the presenter and the peers alike.

Stresses You Might Encounter

Each person deals with stress in different ways. Some people hide stress well so even the most observant person can't recognize it. Others respond in self-protective ways that can be counter-productive to supervision. For instance:

Group members move into consultation before presenter is ready, so presenter feels ambushed or unheard. If you recognize that this has happened, do not be afraid to redirect the session back to supervision. It is okay to interrupt the speaker, and gently remind the group that it is off-track. It is also very helpful to affirm the speaker by addressing any emotion you recognize.

Group members want the presenter to explore feelings about an issue that presenter judges to be sinful or secret. Presenter refuses to discuss it. If so, address the refusal. Ask about what causes such a response (within the presenter.) Your job is to help the presenter discover what drives such a response. Self-evaluation in this area might help the presenter deepen self-awareness.

A group member challenges presenter's reasoning or decision either overtly or without knowing it so presenter feels attacked or accused. This is a common aspect of supervision, especially with new spiritual directors. They do not yet understand or appreciate how the process works. Perhaps they don't have enough self-awareness to clarify any feelings they have. You can assist such a presenter by calling out what you see, mentioning any defensive posture or words, and assuring the person that you mean no harm.

Presenter doesn't trust the group to keep pain private, so presenter grows defensive and defiant, and labels that response 'private' and refuses to discuss. Once you uncover this reason for silence on the part of a presenter, you as peer member are missioned with helping reiterate the "rules" for the group – all is private and will not be discussed outside of the session. Over time, if your group keeps this rule, peer members become more trusting.

Presenter wants to be liked by everyone. Presenter dislikes hard questions or self-disclosure (others may see presenter flaws or sins) and avoids such personal areas, either passively through avoiding or actively through aggression. Again, your job as peer is to notice. Notice and then bring your observations to the session. Use active listening. Express what you see and hear in the presenter, both words and actions.

If you examen each of these issues, you might notice that each focuses on self-protection of the ego. But when we focus more on self-protection than on finding truth or embracing humility, supervision can't be productive.

Your job as supervisor then, becomes more challenging, but not impossible.

- Pray
- Listen to what the person is saying and ask for a deeper explanation.
- If you notice resistance, switch to meta-speak. Ask about the presenter's response to the question rather than trying to get an answer to a question.

Your job as supervisor is to ensure that the supervised person can express responses and emotions honestly. This is a HUGE request, that is so out of the ordinary that it intimidates most people. Don't be harsh. Don't expect people to learn this quickly. Don't expect people to stay unemotional. They will feel torn, dissected and scrutinized even when the group does not intend those responses. Be aware. Be ready for such responses. Redirect any tense conversation back to the tension you feel. Where is it coming from, within the presenter? Find that out and you will discover a wealth of information about the person, along with helping allay fears.

Temptations

First Temptation

The first temptation of Jesus appeals to our need for power and control over our lives and environment.[62] Of course we all have a need to succeed, to achieve, and accomplish. Fr. Cleveland writes, "The danger arises when we base our identity and self-worth on this ability rather than on our inherent dignity and worth as human beings. We might try to earn the approval of God, self, and others based on our achievements."[63]

If you discover that your need for approval from your supervisory peer group members or your directee, or you are wanting more control over the sessions, perhaps your need for control or approval are getting in the way of your honesty or depth. Embrace your humility and mention it to the group.

Here's an example.

Spiritual Director Gloria brought this session to supervision with a directee, Miriam, an emotional mother who was forgetful and overwhelmed with her busy life. Gloria felt great concern for Miriam and wanted to help her to pray more and better.

Miriam: You know how I'm always praying to do God's will, asking for my purpose. He showed me I am more than follower. I'm His daughter! I reached out with my hands like this (demonstrating with extended arms) and offered Jesus my heart. (More tears.)

Gloria: In the past we have talked about ways to counter temptation to stay in bed and not pray. But His Precious Daughter who's offered her heart sounds like prayer may no longer be a task to complete but time spent just loving!

Miriam: I didn't think of it that way. I'm just not a morning person. Never have been. Oh, I remember I wanted to ask you about some materials you gave me. I can't recall the title, but I liked it.

Notice that the spiritual director Gloria was focused on making sure Miriam was praying the "right way," and at the right time. As a result, Gloria completely missed Miriam's amazing emotional experience of being called Daughter by Jesus! She did not comment on the tears or on the gesture. She did not spend time helping Miriam celebrate this amazing experience. As a result, Miriam jumped out of feeling and experiencing back into thinking. She begins evaluating her biological clock and the materials she received instead.

Had Gloria been attentive to the Spirit in this moment, she could have helped Miriam explore that experience more deeply and helped her celebrate God's great gift of love.

Second Temptation

During the second temptation, the devil took Jesus to a high parapet of the temple and goaded him to jump so that angels could catch him. If Jesus would do as the devil tempted, the Devil promised that Jesus would be an instant star. This would impress everyone and would glorify Christ.

But to be the star or the important one is not the way of Christ. On the contrary, Jesus told his followers that his way would be hard. It would include our own cross and require sacrifice, not glory. Each peer is asked to be Christ-like. This is why, in spiritual direction and in supervision, we are asked to step away from the limelight and refuse to be the guru, the "know-it-all" truth-sayer, or the solution-maker, and turn down the temptation to instruct or give solutions

For example, when a directee comes to an impasse and can't decide how to proceed, he might ask, "What should I do?" In order to assist the directee without giving solutions, you as spiritual director could answer, "What do you feel called to do?"

When a directee says, "I'm confused." You as spiritual director can answer, "Tell me more about that confusion," or give a summary of what you've heard the directee say rather than try to solve the problem.

Third Temptation

During the third temptation of Christ, the devil took Jesus to a mountain and showed him the kingdoms of the world. The devil offered them all to Jesus in exchange for worship. We humans are often tempted in this same way. We own stuff and want the accolades that come with that stuff. It is possible to let house, car, clothes, status, education, family, haircut, wisdom, knowledge, or anything else fill us with pride. And desire for accolades concerning those possessions can keep a person from recognizing or accepting God's esteem and accolades. Giving in to this temptation takes a person into the Evil Standard.

Even as you strive to follow Jesus, you might fall into believing that stuff makes you important. The temptation to protect what you own - self-esteem, pride, honor, knowledge - can grab you during supervision and take you out of the Standard of Christ.

In 1 Tim 6:10, St. Paul warns: "People who long to be rich are a prey to temptation; they get trapped into all sorts of foolish and dangerous ambitions which eventually plunge them into ruin and destruction. The love of money is the root of all evils..."[64]

In his book, **Awakening Love**, Fr. Cleveland writes that, "We also have psychological possessions in the realm of intellect and will. Knowledge is good but can easily become a source of pride... Having all the facts, inside information, or good advice to offer others gives us self-satisfaction, and an exalted image of ourselves. We hang our degrees on the wall and display our credentials and titles. Even our spiritual possession – our abilities and the graces we received – can become a means by which we elevate our self-worth." [65]

In the case of supervision, possessions that affect our way of acting might be knowledge, understanding, or experience. These, of course, are positive traits, and are not evil or excessive in and of themselves. But as St. Paul warns, love of any possession, even an inner one, can provide a false sense of security or self-esteem, and can lead a person toward the Standard of Evil.

To inspire us to remain true to our authentic selves, St. Ignatius Loyola tells us that the Standard of Evil includes riches, honor, and pride, and Ignatius exhorts us to ask for the grace to be received "under His standard, first in the highest poverty... in bearing insults and wrongs, thereby to imitate Him better, leading to humility. (see Sp.Ex.136-147)

Cleveland goes on to say, "Because of our temptation to identify ourselves with these goods extrinsic to ourselves, we must forcefully and decisively resist the temptation by acting against them. In this highest spiritual poverty we find our true selves."[66]

As Christian Spiritual Directors, it is our mission to help our directees embrace the Standard of Christ in a deeper way each day of their lives. This Standard includes poverty, humility, and humiliation. We cannot do this unless we ourselves learn to embrace the cross of Christ and live in his love. That is why every Spiritual Director who feels stress during supervision must stop to appreciate and recognize the most important aspect of supervision: self-exploration. Your job of assisting those you direct to grow in the Standard of Christ cannot be accomplished if you, yourself, refuse to embrace poverty of spirit, humility, and humiliation. *You cannot lead where you will not go.*

Supervision isn't punishment. It's not done to torture you or treat you badly. It isn't set up to embarrass or humiliate you. But there will be times when you might still feel embarrassed or humiliated (hopefully not tortured) during supervision.

Your job as presenter is to notice what is happening in your own spirit. If you feel uncomfortable or stressed, say so as soon as you notice it. Your peers need to know what is happening within you so that they have an opportunity to help you overcome your stress, assure you of their love for you, and protect your confidentiality. And as peer group member, you are commissioned to notice the emotional responses of others and discuss as needed.

If you are not able or willing to share your negative emotions during supervision, and not willing to learn to do so, then perhaps spiritual direction is not your gift or calling.

Questions

1. What stresses do I experience in relation to supervision>
2. How much do I trust the members of my team? Why?
3. How do I feel about sharing negative emotions or embarrassing issues with my supervisory team?

4. What am I tempted with in relation to supervision and spiritual direction? How can I allow God to help me overcome that temptation?

19   Consultation

As a presenter, after receiving insight into yourself during supervision, you might also need training or instruction on how to direct or improve spiritual direction skills in each situation.

As a peer supervisor, when you recognize that a person does not know and cannot figure out how to proceed and needs advice, tools, or examples to improve their spiritual direction session, there is a space in supervision for this called consultation.

Instruction

Consultation is a method by which peer team members provide concrete instruction and ways to improve spiritual direction to the presenter. When you as peer supervisor give instruction and/or techniques that assist the spiritual director with a spiritual direction session, you are providing consultation. This instruction might be given at the request of the spiritual director, or it could be given when you recognize that a particular way of proceeding might assist the presenter in the future. Consultation helps the spiritual director learn new ways of listening, speaking, or relating and gains more freedom to discover God for self and others.

Skill

Consultation is a skill that takes practice. It is less giving advice and more about sharing wisdom or experience. Before you consider consultation, use supervision to gain a deeper understanding of what the presenter needs and understands about self. Use the supervision session to help the presenter clarify where God is leading. Trust that God is working in the heart of the presenter during supervision so that peers won't need to provide any consultation.

Humility

Consultation requires humility from peer team members as well as the presenter. Consult with care, in a sensitive, face-saving manner. No one likes to be bossed, belittled, or scolded, or treated like a child. And none of these methods assist the presenter in growing or improving spiritual direction. Consultation should **never** be used to manipulate the presenter into thinking, feeling, or praying as you want or expect.

Here's an example.

Carly, an intern, was directing a woman who practiced a different faith than her own.

"I didn't understand the particular devotions my directee had, so I asked her to explain and enlighten me," Carly wrote in her verbatim. "She seemed happy to instruct me in her faith, and I was glad to hear about it. The directee spent most of the spiritual direction hour discussing what she believed and why."

The supervision team explored Carly's affect in relation to the spiritual direction session. Near the end, a peer said, "I'll switch to consultation now. Your time spent on learning about your directee's faith life reduced her spiritual direction time. This is not fair to either you or her. What could you have done differently to focus on her spiritual life?"

Carly replied, "I thought I was focusing on her spiritual life – at least her faith life. I thought that if I had her educate me, I'd be able to direct her better. What could I have done differently?"

"I see," the peer said. "So you felt a need to understand her faith better. I understand that. But for you to assist her growth and maintain the correct boundary between you and your directee, I suggest you turn to someone other than your directee to educate you on those spiritual practices. This will keep the relationship balanced and prevent her from seeing you as student in this relationship."

When to Consult

Consultation is best done at the end of the supervision. This is important and serves several purposes:

1) Instruction or problem solving is kept separate from the supervision.
2) The supervision team has time to explore and clarify the presenter's situation in depth so they understand better how to proceed.
3) Through the supervision session, as the presenter deepens understanding of values and needs that drove the conversation, the presenter may solve the issue, and consultation might not be needed. (This is the best outcome, since people take their own advice much better than they take anyone else's.)
4) The presenter gains a better understanding of personal needs and what skill to ask for from the peer group members.

In any given session, you might be tempted to think that the presenter needs instruction about how to proceed as you are discussing it. Or you suddenly realize you are giving advice rather than supervision. At this point it is important for you to stop talking and start praying.

Ask God if it's time to switch to consultation. If not, interrupt yourself and return to supervision.

If you feel called to continue into consultation, announce to the group you have done so.

If you aren't sure whether you should continue into consultation, err on the side of caution. Stop consultation and return to supervision.

Consultation VS. Supervision

It is important for you as supervisor to know the difference between consultation and supervision.

Both supervision and consultation focus on the presenter.

Supervision takes the raw material of a direction session and uses it to evaluate what affect, value, need, or Standard, <u>IN THE PRESENTER,</u> was triggered and why.

Consultation takes the material from supervision and uses it to help the presenter develop skills and learn new ways of proceeding that will facilitate spiritual direction. Consultation focuses on what technique can help and how to use it to improve spiritual direction.

How to Consult

If you feel called to move into consultation, remember that you are not the guru, the expert, or the teacher. You are a peer who loves unconditionally, a trusted friend who acts out of love. You are missioned to give consultation only when you know God is calling you to it.

When you switch from supervision to consultation, acknowledge the switch aloud. Say something like, "I have just switched to consultation. The focus is now on technique and how to proceed rather than your affect and experience."

We have found that the most effective method for consultation is role playing. To do this, assign a peer to act as the spiritual director, while the presenter acts as the directee. The presenter rereads the section of the verbatim where consultation is needed. Then, the spiritual director peer team member goes off script and shows what to say and how to say it.

For example, a spiritual director who was also a Christian therapist, brought a session to supervision concerning possible demonic influence. His directee said she felt attacked by evil spirits. The director wasn't sure if it was true or if his directee was delusional. Her actions and comments suggested it could have been either. With supervision, he realized that he felt uncomfortable in her presence and sometimes even forgot to pray with her. He also had been shortening the sessions. He said he didn't feel "safe" when talking with her. As he discussed his reactions, he realized he was acting in ways that were not normal for him. "How can I address her fears?"

Before the group moved to consultation, the director began to understand the tension he was experiencing between his roles of spiritual director and therapist. Supervision gave him the opportunity to consider this tension aloud, and pinpoint where it was coming from within his spirit. When he realized that he could trust God completely, he let go of his desire to "fix" the directee, and answer his own consultation question.

In another example, a spiritual director wanted help her directee spend more time in prayer. "I want to help my directee draw closer to Christ," she wrote for her statement of intent. "My directee doesn't say much, so I'm guessing she isn't praying."

In supervision the director discovered that she herself was uncomfortable with silence in the spiritual direction sessions. She didn't know what to do when the directee was silent. The team roll-played the scenario with her.

During supervision, we clarify director feelings, responses, God's actions using certain specific aspects of a direction session. It's important to clarify what the problem is before we can find any solution. So, we listen to what the director says in relation to the direction session. The supervised person can decide what the experience means and why it happened, as he or she looks within. You, as a member of the supervisory group don't "fix" the directee, or provide a better way to ask questions unless asked.

If a supervised person is truly confused about how to proceed after exploring the experience and affect, if they don't know, or can't discover it through the supervision, that's when consultation can be used.

During Consultation, any member of the supervisory group can explain or teach a specific technique to help the spiritual director understand more fully how to proceed.

Consultation can be done by instruction, roleplaying, or both. Instruction is useful, but roleplaying is frequently more beneficial. Roleplaying helps a group embody the adage for fiction writers: "show don't tell." To accomplish this, one team member and the spiritual director who is being supervised replay a conversational section of the verbatim conversation. The supervisor takes the place of the director. The supervised spiritual director takes the place of the directee and answers for the directee. The spiritual director should try, to the best of his or her ability, to answer in a way like what the directee might answer.

As the roleplaying team member alters the focus of the session by changing the questions, the supervisee sees first-hand how the conversation shifts from the direction it originally went to the direction towards God.

Effective supervisors bring every role-play consultation to God. How do we do this? The process is simple but not always easy. As you participate in any supervision, listen for the emotions that the retreatant brings, or in this case, the spiritual director talking about the retreatant, and capitalize on those.

The following is a small portion of a dialog that a spiritual director brought to supervision.

Directee: I want to talk to you about the ruminations I've been having all week, but I'm scared that sharing them will make things worse. I think I should stay quiet and heal on my own.

Director Affect: Begging God for his help during this session. The sense of spiritual warfare is strong.

Director: I hear how difficult this is for you and how fears keep you bound. Tell me about the punishment you think will happen if you share these things aloud.

Director Affect: My heart goes out to this woman. She is oppressed by lies that fill her mind. I can feel the weight of her pain. I want my words to be life-giving to her.

In supervision, supervisors noticed that the feelings of the directee were not explored in this exchange. We asked, "Tell us about your jumping from the feelings of the directee to what she thought?"

"I didn't think she could talk about those feelings and didn't want to ask her. It felt too invasive somehow. Maybe I thought I'd trip her into deeper depression or something."

With her agreement, we proceeded into role-playing consultation. Now in the role of the directee, the spiritual director repeated,

Directee: *I want to talk to you about the ruminations I've been having all week, but I'm scared that sharing it will make things worse. I think I should stay quiet and heal on my own.*

A team member, acting as the spiritual director, said, ***"Tell me more about your fear and concern about being punished."***

The director, now acting as her directee, took a few moments to think about an answer. ***"As a child, I was punished for honesty, especially if it wasn't what my mother wanted to hear. It still scares me that I might be punished for telling the truth. But I don't want to lie. So, I just stay quiet. I keep trying to heal on my own… but I don't seem to."***

Supervisor Director (*giving a summary to clarify along with some optimistic feedback*): "Amazing. As I listen, I hear you say that you've come to a clearer understanding of your inner self. You know that you are afraid. You also realize that you can't rise above the fear or heal on your own. Did I get that right?"

Directee: "Yes. You got it."

Supervisor Director (bringing in God): "*These are wonderful insights that God has given you. What does God say to you about them?*"

Directee: "*I do believe God is offering me help. I am just afraid of making the wrong choices and making things worse.*"

Supervisor Director: "*What would it be like to let go and let God lead you, tell you what to do each moment. What if you just took a leap and put your whole life in God's hands? Can you trust God that much?*"

In this example, the focus of the conversation changed from what the person feared to the fear itself, and how God works through fear. This is what a consulting group can do for a spiritual director.

Summary

In all you do or say during supervision or consultation, whether you are the presenter or a supervisor, keep the conversation focused on Christ. Whenever the conversation drifts toward trying to solve problems for the directee, all members of the group must stay vigilant to bring the focus back on the spiritual director.

In consultation as with supervision, each member of the group must commit to honesty. Remember you are called to hear the voice of God in the session and speak the truth in love. It is in the more difficult, personal, or emotional subjects and emotions that God reveals gifts and graces that we might otherwise miss.

Help and Support – When we practice non-judgmental, active listening, we help others in the group do the same. In the Spiritual Exercises of St. Ignatius, we explore and deepen our understanding of what it means to love like God. And in supervision, we are called to love in that way – without rancor, without judgement, and with love. Practice doing so at every session. Risk being real.

You as supervisor show respect for the others in the group by expecting them to be open and self-reflective. The purpose of supervision is not to 'accomplish' the process. Nor is it to show how smart anyone is. The point, of course, is to help the spiritual director grow in the ability to love, respond, notice and facilitate God's presence in another person. Dishonesty for any reason, especially to preserve self-image, is never useful in supervision.

If you challenge dishonesty in another, in the person being supervised, your job as supervisor is to do it with love and hope, trusting that the other want to change. When you risk being real, you will help others to follow your lead and do likewise.

We as spiritual directors are called to be strong in Christ. This means we are willing to change when called to do so. We are willing to listen and let others speak. We stay vulnerable and see that as a sign of strength. We do all of this while maintaining integrity. This means, I invite others to question my thought process and my assumptions.

Each session of the spiritual direction process should focus on integrity. How can each person in the meeting work to ensure truth, honor, and honesty? You as an individual can help ensure that the group remains true to Christian principles in every part of the process. Be open to allowing others to question your reasoning, judgement, or intentions.

As you work toward such integrity for your own actions and then in the broader group, take time to allow God to speak. When you don't know what to say or how to stay it, stop and pray. Allow God to speak to you. Your job is to find the truth, not just opinions. Don't settle and just agree to disagree. Find solutions. Then, give solutions in consultation when needed.

Be willing to change. Let your opinion be influenced by others. See vulnerability as strength.

Following the standard of Christ can be counter-intuitive, uncomfortable, or even scary. Sometimes Christ's Standard challenges supervision peer group members and could generate humility or even humiliation. But this standard also increases openness to God, the spiritual director, and the supervisory group members. Choose to follow Christ and supervision will be enriching and helpful.

20   Conclusion

Supervision melds the art of listening, noticing, and caring love with technique and skills. Like an artist mixes colors on a canvas to create beautiful artwork, supervision mixes love, respect, and trust with thought, prayer, and patience. It could take years for a group to learn and practice it well, but supervision can work well, even at first, if the group is focused on Christ's Standard. It can be learned.

Supervision sessions strengthen everyone. It's a powerful tool.

In smaller groups, confidentiality can be a challenge since directors often know all directees. If you have a small group, you'll have to work harder to keep names and details private.

The good news is, group supervision can be learned.

Be patient with yourself and your group. Take good notes after your direction sessions, paying special attention to your own responses to the conversation. Then trust the Holy Spirit to guide you. It's worth the effort

Appendix

Includes:

Ethical Conduct Guidelines

Supervision meeting Agenda

Spiritual Direction Log Form

Identify Statement of Intent Form

Sample Verbatim Conversation – Paragraph form

Sample Verbatim Conversation – Chart form

Supervision Presentation Form

About the Author

Ethical Conduct Guidelines

Ethical conduct flows from God's love for us. Each spiritual director is called to show reverence to directed persons as well as to the peer group members through action and intention. To do this, we are called to follow the standard of Christ, which includes poverty, humility, and humiliation.

These guidelines will hopefully inspire you as peer supervisor and as a spiritual director to strive for integrity, responsibility, and faithfulness in your ministry and provide a God-centered service of others.

Spiritual Director's Personal Growth

Spiritual directors assume responsibility for their personal growth. This means they pray daily to know God and themselves more intimately. They practice spiritual discernment to know God's desire for them, and they practice their faith, to know their community and participate in it. Spiritual directors also need to be in spiritual direction themselves.

Spiritual directors engage in ongoing formation and continuing education. They regularly discern their continued call to ministry and improve their spiritual direction abilities by deepening their understanding of such things as sacred scripture, theology, psychology, spiritual direction techniques, active listening, and more.

Spiritual directors develop their ability to direct others. To do this, they participate in regular supervision practice, training, and education. They also develop their understanding of issues that might interfere with good spiritual direction. These include transference, countertransference, prior emotional wounds, pride, disordered attachments, and any other issue that might arise during a spiritual direction session.

Spiritual directors meet their own needs and care for their self and spirituality outside of the spiritual direction relationship in a variety of ways. They also recognize that they have limits. They prayerfully discern new commitments and other decisions to prevent burnout.

Spiritual Director and Directee

During one of the first few meetings with a directee, a spiritual director initiates a conversation to establish understanding about the nature of spiritual direction, the role of each party, how long and how often the spiritual direction sessions will be, any compensation, and how to end the relationship.

Spiritual directors maintain the confidentiality and privacy of the spiritual directee and make sure all information about a session is kept confidential. Hold every session in a setting that does not compromise the relationship.

Spiritual directors should learn and follow their state's legal requirements in relation to reporting any abuse or harm they discover to adults, children, or anyone else, including your directee.

Spiritual directors honor the dignity of the spiritual directee in many ways. They respect the spiritual directee's values, culture, conscience, and spirituality. They refrain from discussing motives, experiences, or relationships out of curiosity. Rather, they ask for details on motives, experiences, or relationships only when necessary to understand further what the person is trying to express in relation to prayer.

Spiritual Director and Community

Spiritual directors maintain relationships with colleagues and get written releases and/or permission from directees when specific information needs to be shared.

Spiritual directors practice communal discernment. They participate in regular supervision and remain accountable to peers and directees. They work to deepen their relationship and trust in their team or supervisor.

Spiritual directors represent their organization accurately, so they remain open and honest with the directee and others about process and expectations. They tell the truth about qualifications and affiliations and seek ways to assist spiritually those who are underserved.

They try to live in an ecologically responsible and sustainable manner and respect all persons.

© E. Tomaszewski

Negative Feeling List

Abandoned	Disconsolate	Horrified	Self-conscious
Abhorrent	Discontented	Humiliated	Separate
Afraid	Disdainful	Ignored	Shocked
Alarmed	Disgusted	Impotent	Shy
Alienated	Disillusioned	Indignant	Sick
Annoyed	Disliked	Inhibited	Sullen
Antagonistic	Dismal	Lethargic	Suspicious
Anxious	Dismayed	Listless	Tempted
Apprehensive	Dissatisfied	Loathed	Tense
Aversion	Distant	Mad	Terrified
Avoided	Disturbed	Marginalized	Threatened
Bad	Dreadful	Miffed	Timid
Baffled	Edgy	Mistreated	Tired
Bashful	Embarrassed	Mixed up	Trapped
Bewildered	Enmity	Moody	Troubled
Bitter	Envious	Nervous	Uncomfortable
Bored	Estranged	Outcast	Unhappy
Confused	Fatigued	Panicky	Unloved
Contemptuous	Fed-up	Perplexed	Unpopular
Degraded	Forlorn	Pitiful	Upset
Dejected	Frightened	Provoked	Wearied
Depressed	Frustrated	Puzzled	Worried
Despised	Futile	Resentful	Worthless
Detested	Gloomy	Sad	
Disappointed	Hate	Scared	

Positive Feelings List

Accomplished	Confident	Happy	Regarded
Active	Consoled	Heroic	Relaxed
Admired	Content	Hopeful	Relieved
Adored	Courageous	Hyper	Respected
Adventurous	Deliberate	Idolized	Secure
Affectionate	Delighted	Important	Sensitive
Alert	Determined	Infatuated	Strong
Alive	Direct	Inspired	Sure
Amazed	Eager	Intelligent	Sympathetic
Amused	Effervescent	Interested	Tender
Animated	Elated	Jolly	Turned on
Anticipating	Empathetic	Joyful	Untroubled
Appealing	Enchanted	Keen	Valiant
Approved	Enthusiastic	Kind	Vibrant
Arduous	Esteemed	Liked	Virtuous
At ease	Excited	Loved	Wanted
Attractive	Exuberant	Lustful	Warm
Audacious	Firm	Optimistic	Wide awake
Awed	Fond	Patient	Wild
Benevolent	Friendly	Patient	Worthy
Bold	Glad	Peaceful	Worthy
Brave	Good	Peaceful	Yearning
Brilliant	Graceful	Pitying	Zealous
Cared for	Gracious	Pleased	
Comfortable	Gratified	Proud	
Concerned	Gutsy	Radical	

© E. Tomaszewski

Spiritual Direction Log Form

Record each directee session using this format. Then, you can use these notes to help you prepare your supervision paper.

Director's name: _____   Session Date: _____
Length of session: _____   Interview #: _____
Directee Code name: _____

1. Describe your relationship with the directee in general. What do you sense to be the response or impression of the directee toward you? Can you connect this to any response or behavior (verbal or non-verbal) of yours?

2. Briefly note the session's focus. Include content, themes, religious experience of the directee, and other relevant issues.

3. What was the directee most comfortable discussing or exploring in depth?

4. What issues that you brought up did the directee avoid, ignore, or deflect?

5. Do you think the directee became engaged in the experience of God during the session?

6. How would you assess the directee considering the themes and major issues you discussed with him or her? How do you want to respond in future meetings?

7. Add any further understanding about the dynamics of the session and/or the dynamics of the directee's relationship with God.

Identifying Your Statement of Intent Form

Use this form to help you identify what you were experiencing during a spiritual direction session. Pay particular attention to any feelings that took you from God or directee to self.

Director's name: _____ Session Date: _____
Length of session: _____ Session #: _____
Directee Code name: _____

- What is your impression of the directee toward you during this session?
- What was your directee most comfortable discussing or exploring in depth?
- What was your response to any issues that your directee avoided, ignored or deflected.

- Can you connect this to any response or behavior (verbal or non-verbal) of yours?
- What was your response to any comfort, avoidance, or deflection in your directee?
- Based on the dynamics of the session and/or the dynamics of the directee's relationship with God, what do you need to discover about yourself and how you responded during this session?

© E. Tomaszewski

Sample Verbatim Paragraph Style

R 1: I prayed about God creating me moment by moment and it comforted me. I like that I am constantly being created.
MY AFFECT: I'm feeling a <u>bit scattered</u>. I got the room ready, then totally forgot L was coming I feel <u>embarrassed</u> about my "senior moment and feel <u>humbled</u> by it.

D 1: Tell me more.
MY AFFECT: I'm <u>engaged</u>, I'm feeling <u>ready</u>, on task.

R 2: I used to live in a fancy house with lots of things. Now I live in a tiny house with few things. I used to be with people all the time, now I'm mostly alone. It's a time of transition but I do have more time with God. I'm changing, and I can see God's hand in it.
MY AFFECT:. I feel <u>open</u> and <u>helpful</u>. Want to help discover where God fits into it. I feel <u>glad</u> that she can see God in this.

D 2. What's that like for you, to have more time for God? To be changing with God's help?
MY AFFECT: I feel <u>careful</u>. Want to ensure I'm not assuming something that isn't true, and to allow her to explore this. I feel <u>concerned</u> I might assume or miss something. Want to allow her to explore this. Feel <u>grateful</u> to God for his presence.

R 3. Well, sometimes it's scary to be alone, but I've been trying to take more time to pray and fit God in. And I think that I am called to do SOMETHING, but I don't know what it is yet. It's hard to wait to find out. But I'm willing to wait on God.
MY AFFECT: I feel <u>humbled</u> by her admission of impatience. I feel <u>comfortable</u> to allow God to reveal in God's own time what the directee is called to do.

D3 Sounds like you have lots of emotions going on – I heard you say "lonely, scared," and that you are "waiting on God." That's a great thing, to wait for God.
MY AFFECT: *L isn't always able to isolate her feelings, so I try to point them out when I hear them. I'm <u>excited</u> about her openness to waiting on God.*

R 4 But it's so hard to do. I just want to get on with things. I feel so unproductive. I don't like waiting but I realize I'm learning how to wait. I'm willing to wait.
MY AFFECT: *I feel <u>supportive</u> and <u>open</u> to what God is doing.*

D4 Ah, yes, I hear you. It's very hard to do. It takes patience. And I see you exercising that patience.
MY AFFECT: *I feel <u>hopeful and inspired.</u> Want to affirm her in her efforts and patience. I understand the challenge of waiting on God.*

R 5. Really? I'm glad, because I thought I was being impatient.
MY AFFECT: *<u>Gratified</u> that she can see her actions in a new light.*

D 5: You seem surprised about that.
MY AFFECT: *I feel <u>careful</u> not to assume anything. I want to confirm that I am reading her correctly.*

R 6: Yes, I thought I was impatient because I want results. And I don't like to wait. But I do see that I'm not forcing them [the results] I'm waiting. My friends and my lawyer all tell me to wait. And now even God in my prayer tells me!

Sample Verbatim Conversation Chart Style

DIRECTOR AFFECT	CONVERSATION
I'm feeling scattered. I got the room ready, then totally forgot L was coming. I feel embarrassed about my "senior moment." It reminds me of how human I am.	Directee 1: I prayed about God creating me moment by moment and I got a lot out of it. I believe I am constantly being created; it comforted me.
I'm engaged, I'm now on task.	Director 1: Tell me more.
I feel <u>open</u> and <u>helpful</u>. Want to help discover where God fits into it. I feel <u>glad</u> that she can see God in this.	R 2: I used to live in a fancy house with lots of things. Now I live in a tiny house with few things. I used to be with people all the time, now I'm mostly alone. It's a time of transition but I do have more time with God. I'm changing, and I can see God's hand in it.
I feel <u>careful</u>. Want to ensure I'm not assuming, and to allow her to explore this. I felt <u>concerned</u> I might assume or miss something. Want to allow her to explore this. I feel <u>grateful</u> to God for his	D 2. What's that like for you, to have more time for God?
I feel <u>humbled</u> by her admission of impatience and <u>comfortable</u> to allow God to reveal in God's own time what the directee is called to do.	R 3. Well, sometimes it's scary to be alone, but I've been trying to take more time to pray and fit God in. And I think that I am called to do SOMETHING, but I don't know what it is yet. So it's hard to wait to find out. But I'm willing to wait on God.

DIRECTOR AFFECT	CONVERSATION
L isn't always able to isolate her feelings, so I try to point them out when I hear them. I'm excited about her openness to	D3 Sounds like you have lots of emotions going on – I heard you say "lonely, scared," and that you are "waiting on God." That's a great thing, to wait for God.
I feel supportive and open to what God is doing. Want to affirm her in her efforts and patience.	R 4 But it's so hard to do. I just want to get on with things. I feel so unproductive. I don't like waiting but I realize I'm learning how to wait. I'm willing to wait.
I understand the challenge of waiting on God but I feel hopeful and inspired that God can assist. Want to affirm her in her efforts and patience.	D4 Ah, yes, I hear you. It's hard to do. It takes patience. And I see you exercising that patience.
Hopeful that I can help her see what I see - that she was letting God speak and she was patient.	R 5. Really? I'm glad, because I thought I was being impatient.
I feel careful not to assume. I want to confirm that I am reading her	D 5: You seem surprised about that.
	R 6: Yes, I thought I was impatient because I want results. And I don't like to wait. But I do see that I'm not forcing them [the results] I'm waiting. My friends and my lawyer all tell me to wait. And now even God in my prayer tells me to wait!

© E. Tomaszewski

Supervision Presentation Form (for presenter)

Today's Date	Directee's Code Name
Director's Name	Date of Conversation

Please write your answers to the following questions and include a verbatim, written in one of the two formats shown above. If possible, send your paper to the group before your supervision meeting.

Give a brief biography of the directee. (***What do your peers need to know to help them understand this situation better? Share only public information here.***)

Statement of Intent
Identify specifically why you are bringing this session to supervision, and what you want your team to assist you with. Answer this statement: I want my peer supervision team to:

Verbatim
Attach verbatim. During the supervision session, read the verbatim with another person if possible, each taking directee or director role. Then continue reading your responses to the following questions.

1. What was the main experience that the directee brought to the spiritual direction session? (This could be anything - a

confusing or amazing prayer experience; any strong emotion such as enthusiasm, fear, consolation, anger; or triumphs/struggles in any area.)

2. Which rules of discernment did you use or discuss during this session?
   a. Please explain how you used the discernment rule(s) and how this helped (or didn't).

3. How did my directee and I discover/explore God's presence in this session?

4. What physical signs or body language occurred in the directee or me? (Tears, nervous habits, closing eyes, wringing hands, twisting tissue, tapping feet, etc.)
   a. Were you able to ask the directee about these signs, and what they meant to the directee? If so, what did I learn?
   b. How did this affect the session?

5. What were my feelings:
   - At the beginning of the session?
   - At the end of the session?
   - To what do I attribute the difference?
   - Where did I experience the strongest feeling (name it) and why?

6. What issues (if any) did I experience in the direction session that I would like to consult with others in this group to give me advice or instruction (consultation)?

Supervision Meeting Agenda

For each meeting, assign one facilitator and one presenter (not the same person.) Rotate so each member of the group gets a chance to facilitate and present.

Opening (1 minute) *Facilitator reminds the group of intent, focus, and attitude of meeting.* "I want to remind you that the focus of both the presentation and discussion should be on presenter, not the directee. The intent of this meeting is to be open to the Holy Spirit. Also, this process is confidential. Please don't discuss anything said here outside of this meeting.

1) **Prayer** (1 min.) "We will take about 1-2 minutes of silent prayer before we start."
2) **Presentation** (up to 15 min.) - Other members listen silently while presenter reads prepared paper.
3) **Clarification Questions** (5 min.) Clarify, don't elaborate.
4) **Silent prayer, reflection, and writing** - (3-5 min.)
5) **Discussion** and questions (up to 30 min.)
6) **Consultation** - Bring any shift to consultation or problem-solving to the attention of the group. Recognize and discuss issues of technique or process. Identify and assist the director in recognizing, addressing, or dealing with issues.
7) **Silent Prayer** (1-2 min.)
8) **Evaluate** the meeting (5 min.)
    a) How well did we stay focused on the presenter as opposed to the directee? Any places we were off-track?
    b) What Fruits of the Spirit did we use, explore, or deepen? *(Charity, joy, peace, patience, kindness, goodness, generosity, gentleness, faithfulness, modesty, self-control, and chastity)*
9) How did presenter/peers feel about the meeting?
10) **Prayer** (1 min.)- silent or verbal.

About the Author

Ellen Tomaszewski has been involved in the Spiritual Exercises in Everyday Life (SEEL) Ignatian Exercises 19th Annotation, since 1987. She became a spiritual director in the program in 1989 and has been active in this ministry ever since.

Ellen loves the Spiritual Exercises and especially discernment, because it helps her (and so many others) identify God's desire. In doing so, discernment takes the guilt out of saying no, and adds the joy into saying yes. Ellen continues to be very excited about prayer, and fascinated that God wants us to know him intimately. She wishes that everyone could experience a deep and personal relationship with God. She is excited about bringing the Spiritual Exercises of St. Ignatius to areas that would otherwise not have access such as small towns, remote or rural areas.

The SEEL group in the town where Ellen lives had never had any Jesuit presence, no Jesuit university or others able to assist with the ministry of the Spiritual Exercises. Personal assistance from people who were knowledgeable in the program just wasn't available. And so, out of necessity, Ellen began writing—to record what the group did at the meetings. After her training in Supervision at Mercy Center in Burlingame, CA, Ellen wrote what she learned and included her experience of group supervision with SEEL, into a manual for supervisors called ***Group Supervision, Method and Practice,*** which has expanded to this book.

In between, Ellen has become quite interested in the New Evangelization, especially for very young children. She is writing and publishing a series of board books that teach the basics of the Catholic faith. These include *Articles at Mass* and *Stations of the Cross* so far.

The following books were written for those who want to provide the Spiritual Exercises in Everyday Life but don't have a well-trained staff, or any Jesuit presence in their community. Hopefully they will bless you and your group.

Taking the Exercises to the World—provides group meeting agendas and materials plus organizational charts and schedules needed to run the Spiritual Exercises 19th Annotation smoothly.

Discerning God's Call—Provides meeting agendas and training materials for those discerning if God is calling them to join a Spiritual Exercise program as a spiritual director. This book also includes ethics.

Intern Handbook—Provides meeting agendas and training materials for those who are in their first year of spiritual direction as an intern. This book includes ethics as well as supervision instruction.

Group Supervision Method and Practice— small handbook (36 pages) that provides clear instruction on how to perform supervision as a group to one another. This includes a meeting agenda, instructions on writing the verbatim and supervision paper, what questions to ask, the difference between supervision and consultation, and how to proceed.

Preparation Days Retreat – God Loves ME! 3 Booklet Set

- ***Writing Your Faith Autobiography*** Includes four weeks of daily questions so that a person can complete a faith autobiography by answering one question a day. Includes journal pages for entries. A very easy and simple way to write a faith autobiography. Can be used for the Preparation Days Retreat, or it can stand alone for the Spiritual Exercises, if desired.

- ***Director Handbook*** Includes all instructions, agendas, prayers, and sample presentations needed for five weekly meetings of a retreat on the Preparation Days of the Spiritual Exercises of St. Ignatius 19th Annotation.

- ***Participant Handbook*** Includes readings, group meeting agendas, discussion questions and daily journal pages for a the five-week Preparation Days Retreat.

Ms. Tomaszewski has also written several other non-Ignatian spirituality books. These include:

Toxic, a novel of suspense. In 1971, young single mother Emma Lee Dubois experiences a head injury at work and loses her memory. Without friends or family, this displaced southerner is victimized by her 63-year-old lecherous boss, Leonard Baxter. Six months later, Emma Lee regains enough short-term memory to realize that she's married to the creepy controlling codger; and she's pregnant with his child. As Emma Lee heals, Leonard resorts to lies, manipulation, abuse, and an arsenal of chemicals at his disposal to maintain control. And Emma Lee discovers that escaping from Leonard may be the hardest thing she's ever done.

Rose Colored Glasses How to swallow pride without choking and other motherly tasks. When Katy is born, her eyes jiggle, bounce, cross and squint. Doctors confirm she's visually impaired and color blind, but offer no diagnosis. Worse, her IQ tests half that of normal babies her age. Her mother (author Tomaszewski) is devastated, but determined to find the cause and possibly a cure. This book explores how to let go of the things we grasp and covet, in order to get what we deserve—God's gift of love and life.

***Articles at Mass* board book for the very young Catholic**—Kids and parents alike will appreciate these beautiful, large color photos and short descriptions of items seen during a Roman Catholic Mass. It's the perfect Mass companion for any young child. And it's a great book to read ahead so a child knows what to look for.

***Stations of the Cross* - board book for the very young Catholic -** This striking book for young Catholics prompts delight in the beauty and solemnity of the Stations of the Cross. It also provides a simple Lenten devotion while teaching about sacred art and history of the Stations of the Cross. This is a perfect companion for the Stations of the Cross meditation, and is appropriate for children at Holy Mass any time.

Robin Hood the Just **Picture book.**

Few fairy tales mention faith, let alone religion. But kids need to see characters who are grounded in faith. Robin Hood the Just does so. The story is based on a song from the Middle Ages that tells of Robin Hood going to Mass and praying the rosary during the day, while helping others. Inspired by Pope John Paul II's call to the New Evangelization, Robin Hood the Just is designed to entertain children while letting them see the importance of living the Catholic faith. Published by Tan Books.

21   Endnotes

[1] St. John of the Cross, *The Living Flame of Love, stanza 3, 30,* in *The Collected Works of St. John of the Cross,* eds K. Kavanaugh OCD and O Rodriguez OCD (Washington DC, Institute of Carmelite Studies, 1979), 621

[2] David L. Flemming, SJ, *Draw me Into Your Friendship – The Spiritual Exercises;* page 14 Annotation [15] St. Louis, MO. © 1996

[3] Jerusalem Bible; Doubleday and Company, Garden City, New York. Romans 6:17-18

[4] William A Barry, SJ, *Allowing the Creator to Deal with the Creature,* page 21. Paulist Press New York, © 1994

[5] Willam A Barry, S.J. PhD; Human Development Magazine; Volume Nine, Number 1, Spring 1988.. Page 30.

[6] https://www.vaticannews.va/en/pope/news/2023-03/pope-francis-10-anniversary-interview-swiss-radio-tv-pontificate.html. March 10, 2023

[7] Michael Ivens S.J., *Understanding the Spiritual Exercises*; page 105. Inigo Enterprises Surrey, © 1998; reprinted 2008.

[8] Michael Ivens S.J., *Understanding the Spiritual Exercises*; page 109. Inigo Enterprises Surrey, © 1998; reprinted 2008.

[9] Michael Ivens S.J., *Understanding the Spiritual Exercises*; page 109. Inigo Enterprises Surrey, © 1998; reprinted 2008.

[10] CS Lewis, *Mere Christianity* as quoted on the website Pride and Humility - C.S. Lewis Institute (cslewisinstitute.org)

[11] Colossians 3: 12-15. The Jerusalem Bible; 1969; Doubleday and Company; page 260

[12] David L Fleming, S.J. *Draw me Into Your Friendship, the Spiritual Exercises a Literal Translation and a Contemporary Reading;* page 130.Institute of Jesuit Sources © 1996.

[13] Michael Ivens S.J., *Understanding the Spiritual Exercises*; page 110. Inigo Enterprises Surrey, © 1998; reprinted 2008.

[14] Catechism of the Catholic Church; Pauline St. Paul Books and Media, © 1994; Section 1832.

[15] Rolheiser, Ronald, *The Holy Longing – the search for a Christian Spirituality, page 53.* Image Random House, New York. 1999

[16] Rolheiser, Ronald, *Sacred Fire, page 158.* Image Random House, New York. 2014

[17] *Hearts on Fire – Praying with Jesuits*

[18] Michael Ivens S.J., *Understanding the Spiritual Exercises*; page 226. Inigo

Enterprises Surrey, © 1998; reprinted 2008.
[19] Anthony DeMello *The Way to Love,* Image Books, Doubleday New York, London, Toronto, Sydney, Aukland 1991. Page 85
[20] The Carpenters; *Rainy Days and Mondays* 1971
[21] https://counselling-matters.org.uk/cognitive-behavioural-therapy-cbt/
[22] Beatrice Bruteau Radical Optimism – Practical Spirituality in an Uncertain World. Sentient Publication, LLC, Boulder, CO. p. 47; 2002
[23] New Jerusalem Bible, Matthew 15: 19-20.
[24] Joseph Tetlow, SJ. Choosing Christ in the World page 233
[25] David L. Fleming, S.J., *Draw me Into Your Friendship,* Page 247; © Institute of Jesuit Sources, St. Louis 1998, reprinted 2008.
[26] David L. Fleming, S.J., *Draw me Into Your Friendship*, Pgs 247-259; © Institute of Jesuit Sources, St. Louis 1998, reprinted 2008.
[27] David L. Fleming, S.J., *Draw me Into Your Friendship,* Paragraph [326], Page 257; © Institute of Jesuit Sources, St. Louis 1998, reprinted 2008.
[28] Ronald Rolheiser, *The Holy Longing – The Search for a Christian Spirituality;* Doubleday, A division of Random House Inc. New York, NY. 1999. Page 86.
[29] Cf. Sebastian Moore, *Let this Mind Be in You: The Quest for Identity through Oedipus to Christ.* San Francisco: Harper & Row (Winston), 1985.
[30] https://www.catholicculture.org/commentary/self-esteem-and-love-god/
[31] Fr. Michael Esparza, Self-Esteem Without Selfishness: Increasing Our Capacity for Love. Scepter Press, 2013.
[32] https://en.wikipedia.org/wiki/Humility
[33] The Jerusalem Bible, Doubleday and Company, Garden City, NY. pg 298.
[34] The Jerusalem Bible, Doubleday and Company, Garden City NY pg 1064
[35] IBID page 832
[36] Dr. Orestes A Brownson, *The Moral and Social Influence of Devotion to Mary*; Catholicculture.org
https://www.catholicculture.org/culture/library/view.cfm?id=5860&repos=1&subrepos=0&searchid=2286851
[37] https://www.vaticannews.va/en/pope-francis/mass-casa-santa-marta/2018-01/pope-homily-santa-marta0.html
[38] Kevin O'Brien, JS, *The Ignatian Adventure;* Loyola Press,
[39] Louis J Puhl, S.J. *The Spiritual Exercises of St. Ignatius – based on studies in the language of the autograph.* Loyola University Press, Chicago. 1951. Pg 69
[40] https://www.merriam-webster.com/dictionary/affect

[41] https://www.merriam-webster.com/dictionary/affect
[42] Joseph Tetlow, SJ, Choosing Christ in the World. © 1999 The Institute of Jesuit Sources. St. Louis, MO. Page 240.
[43] Maureen Conroy, R.S.M., Looking into the Well, page 19; Loyola Press, Chicago. © 1995
[44] Ronald B Adler, Russell E. Proctor II, Looking Out Looking In, Wadsworth, Cengage Learning Boston, MA.; 2014 Page 79
[45] https://www.merriam-webster.com/dictionary/empathy
[46] The Jerusalem Bible; Doubleday& Company, Inc. Garden City, NY. 1968 Page 91.
[47] The Jerusalem Bible; Doubleday & Company, Inc. Garden City, NY. 1968. Page 129.
[48] Ronald B. Adler and Russell Proctor II, Looing out Looking In, fourteenth edition. Wadsworth Cengage Learning. 2014. Page 221.
[49] Caso, L, Vrij, A. Mann, s. & DeLeo, G. (2006) Deceptive responses: The imct of verbal and non-verbal countermeasures. *Legal and Criminological Psychology -*, 11, 99-111; Vrig, A. (2004) Why professionals fail to catch lars and how they can improve. *Legal and Criminological Psychology, 9, 159-181.*
[50] Catechism of the Catholic Church - Paragraph # 2690 page 647, Pauline St. Paul Books and Media.Vaticano, 1983
[51] David L. Flemming, SJ, *Draw me Into Your Friendship – The Spiritual Exercises;* page 14 Annotation [15] St. Louis, MO. © 1996.
[52] Ronald Adler, Russell F. Proctor II; Looking Out Looking In, fourteenth edition; Wadsworth Cengage Learning 2014 p.189
[53] Beatrice Bruteau (2002) Radical Optimism – Practical Spirituality in an Uncertain World. Sentient Publication, LLC, Boulder, CO. p. 34
[54] Jordan Peterson. 12 Rules for Life, An Antidote to Chaos; Random House Canada. 2018 p 246
[55] Taken from Rogers, C. R. (1952) "Communication: its Blocking and its Facilitation" *ETC: A Review of General Semantics*, 9, 83-88.
[56] Jordan Peterson. *12 Rules for Life, An Antidote to Chaos*; Random House Canada. 2018
[57] Ronald B Adler, Russell E. Proctor II, Looking Out Looking In, Wadsworth, Cengage Learning Boston, MA.; © 2014 Pg 84
[58] Ronald Adler, Russell F. Proctor II; Looking Out Looking In, fourteenth edition; Wadsworth Cengage Learning 2014 p.189
[59] Goodman G., & Esterly G. Questions – the most popular piece of

language. In J. Stewart (ed.) ***Bridges not Walls*** (5th edition pp. 69-77) New York, McGraw-Hill. (1990)
[60] Ronald B Adler, Russell E. Proctor II, Looking Out Looking In, Wadsworth, Cengage Learning Boston, MA.; © 2014 p. 84
[61] https://www.verywellmind.com/counter-transference-2671577
[62] Gregory Cleveland, OMV. Awakening Love, An Ignatian Retreat with the Song of Songs. Pauline Books and Media, Pauline Books. [2017] Page 164
[63] Gregory Cleveland, OMV. Awakening Love, An Ignatian Retreat with the Song of Songs. Pauline Books and Media, Pauline Books. [2017] Page 164
[64] The Jerusalem Bible, Readers Edition, Doubleday & Company Inc, Garden City, New York. Page 272.
[65] Gregory Cleveland, OMV. Awakening Love, An Ignatian Retreat with the Song of Songs. Pauline Books and Media, Pauline Books. [2017] Page 166
[66] Gregory Cleveland, OMV. Awakening Love, An Ignatian Retreat with the Song of Songs. Pauline Books and Media, Pauline Books. [2017] Page 168

www.ingramcontent.com/pod-product-compliance
Lightning Source LLC
Chambersburg PA
CBHW071700090426
42738CB00009B/1601